Just The Way I Am

— The Ivan Thompson Story —

NOEL I. DAVIDSON

Just The Way I Am

ISBN 1 898787 16 6

AMBASSADOR PRODUCTIONS LTD
Providence House,
16 Hillview Avenue,
Belfast, BT5 6JR,
United Kingdom

Contents

---

1. *Granny* 7
2. *The Flit* 13
3. *A Tract Or A Sixpence* 19
4. *"SNAP!"* 27
5. *The Missing Piece* 35
6. *Released Into Captivity* 43
7. *Wedding And Weeping* 49
8. *The Big Find* 59
9. *"You Will Be In Hell"* 67
10. *The Lady's Choice* 73

11. *It's Later Than You Think* 77

12. *Just As You Are* 85

13. *God's Taximan* 91

14. *First Encounters* 97

15. *The Secret Of Success* 103

16. *It's A Bomb!* 109

17. *Do You Know Where You're Going?* 111

18. *Good News, Bad News* 119

19. *What's Wrong With Us?* 125

20. *Why Take The Risk?* 131

Introduction

As we sat in a Belfast restaurant, my mind was working overtime.

I had come to have a chat with Ivan Thompson and his wife, Sylvia. The idea was that I should hear some incidents from Ivan's life story to decide if his experiences with God would make an interesting chapter in a book of Christian testimonies.

Ivan talked on over the meal. He had much to tell.

There was a baby left without a mother at three months old. There was a kind Granny who took and reared the child.

Then there were the tough times.

His father used to call, from time to time, and give him a new pair of shoes.

Great excitement!

His granny used to take them down to the pawn-shop the next day to obtain a few extra shillings to buy food.

Great disappointment.

A sad decline into a life of petty crime, led eventually to a prison sentence.

There was a tender love story all mixed up in it, too.

Ivan met Sylvia. Ivan liked Sylvia. Ivan married Sylvia.

The young couple were happy together. Well, for a while, at least.

Then Sylvia had a very real experience with God. She was saved.

A marked change became evident in his wife's lifestyle. Ivan laughed at her, and her God and her faith ...

That was, of course, only until God intervened in his life as well ...

The evening progressed and I began to see the picture more clearly. I had been anticipating Ivan's final question for most of the evening and when it came I had the answer ready.

"Do you think there is a chapter for your book of testimonies in there somewhere?" he asked, with a twinkle in his eye.

"I think there is a whole book with a lot of chapters in there, Ivan," was my response.

Sylvia smiled knowingly. She had been sure of that all along.

"Yes," I continued, "it has all the ingredients. Granny, love stuff, hardship, disappointments, God's leading and guiding and miraculous power and the prospect of unending bliss ..."

We then decided that Ivan's life story should be told as a book, so that others could learn of God's wonderful dealings with Ivan, and Sylvia, his wife.

Ivan and I have met often over the past year. As the variety of his experiences were unfolded to me, step by step, incident by incident, two things impressed me.

One. Here is a man who knows what it is to be in daily and meaningful contact with God.

And, two. What a mighty, kind and gracious God we have. A God who could find Ivan Thompson where he was, and bring him to where he is now.

A God who is Love.

It is Ivan's prayer, and mine also, that as you read this book you may be drawn close to God.

May you find, as Paul the apostle, once Saul the persecutor, found out so long ago, and as Ivan the Pastor, once Ivan the mocker, has found out more recently, that:-

"My God shall supply all your need according to his riches in glory by Christ Jesus." Philippians 4:19

1

Granny

The bully glowered across the table at the ten year old boy. It was an eyeball-to-eyeball confrontation.

Pointing down at young Ivan's dinner he said, "I'm taking this. Have you any objections?"

Ivan glanced quickly around the prefabricated building that served as a canteen for Getty Junior School. Not much help there. Everybody was too busy. Chatting, arguing, eating.

He looked back across the table. The intimidator was holding up a clenched fist. And what a fist! It seemed colossal!

Time for a spot of quick thinking. "I would be better to lose my dinner than lose my teeth," reasoned Ivan.

With as casual an approach as he could possibly display in the circumstances, Ivan slid his dinner plate across the table.

"Here, you might as well take it. I don't like it today anyway," he replied.

This was to be the start of a pattern. On whatever day his tormentor decided that he wanted Ivan's dinner, he just came up and took it. No questions asked. Day after day the hungry schoolboy was having nothing at all in School except his bottle of milk at the morning break.

He was too frightened to tell anyone about it, for he knew that reporting it would only make life totally intolerable for him. So he endured the nagging and the hunger.

Ivan Thompson lived with his grandmother.

He had been born into a Christian home, but his mother Ellie had died when he was only three months old. His father was also unwell, and therefore unable to cope with the rearing of two young sons, considering all the care and attention that would be needed.

Jim was four years old. Ivan was only three months.

Granny Myles took brother Jim.

Granny Thompson took baby Ivan.

Just to give their father a break.

There were no visits from the Social Services. No forms to be filled. No legalities.

Ivan's granny had just wrapped him in a shawl and taken him. To rear him.

There was one further complication in this sad situation. Granny didn't have a permanent home to which she could take the baby.

She lived in lodgings.

Sometimes she lived with her sons or her daughters and their families. Occasionally she rented a room for the two of them out of her pension.

Thus it was that Ivan Thompson was growing up on the Shankill Road in Belfast. There were times when he lived in a house with five or six other children. There were other occasions when he and granny would be on their own.

It seemed that there was hardly a street on the Shankill Road, but they had lived in it. Tobergill Street, Hopewell Street, Fifth Street, Belgrave Street, Fortingale Street ...

Granny Thompson had been informed that because of the nomadic nature of their circumstances, Ivan would be granted a free meal in School each day. However, the kind lady was totally unaware that Ivan wasn't now eating even half of the dinners to which he was entitled.

They were staying in Fortingale Street with Aunt Ellen.

Ivan's cousin John and he were about the same age and they trudged back and forward to Getty Junior together.

John often urged Ivan. "You should tell your granny about your dinners. I bet you she would soon go up to School and sort it out!"

There was no way that Ivan was going to tell his granny about it. He certainly didn't want her to have to "sort it out"!

He had a nightmarish vision of hoards of children gathered around him in the playground, chanting

"Ivan brought his granny down ... Ivan brought his granny down ..."

This was a serious handicap to a growing boy. Ivan's granny was extremely good to him. And he loved her. But he couldn't say, "I'll bring my big brother down to you," or, "I'll tell my mother on you," and he WOULDN't say, "I'll get my granny to you!"

So he was bullied. A soft touch. A granny's boy.

One winter evening Aunt Ellen and family, Ivan and granny, were all clustered around the big shiny wooden wireless listening to "Dan Dare". It was one of their favourite programmes. Those who couldn't find a chair to sit on in the tiny room just sat on the hearth rug by the fire.

It was cosy.

Ivan wasn't on a rug. He was sharing a chair, across the room from granny.

He was conscious of her gazing at him. She looked away and then looked back, but Ivan pretended not to notice.

"You're getting very pale, Ivan, son," she said at length. "Are you all right?"

"Oh, I've got a dose of the cold, granny," was the almost-too-ready response.

John decided that it was time she knew the truth. The whole truth.

"That big bully in school takes his dinner," he blurted out.

"He's a-scared of him, granny! and I'm a-scared of him as well!"

Ivan stared angrily at his tell-tale cousin.

"Well, thank you, John!" He yelled across at him.

When he returned his attention to his granny his attitude changed dramatically. He had decided to play the whole thing down.

"To tell you the truth, granny, the big fellow is doing me a favour," he fibbed. "You want to see the dinners! You couldn't eat them!"

After pausing a moment for thought, he added, "Well, I couldn't anyway."

Granny was not impressed. Ivan knew her well enough to know that. But she said no more and he was happy enough to let the matter drop.

On the next day, when the bully-boy was walking home from school, a hand shot out of an alleyway and pulled him in. Just snatched him off the street!

It was granny on the war path!

The ageing little woman in the dark clothes had a fiery spirit.

She had been left a widow at an early age and had raised her own family single-handed.

She was not to be trifled with!

Pinning the by-now-quaking bully against the wall with her left hand, she set the shopping basket that she had been carrying in her right hand, down beside her.

From it she produced a large empty lemonade bottle. One of Cantrell and Cochrane's.

Pressing the bottle against her terrified captive's nose she announced menacingly, "If you take my Ivan's dinner one more time I will break this over your skull! Do you understand that?"

The one-time bully nodded as vigorously as the slowly retreating bottle would permit.

When granny relaxed her grip he fled, suitable chastened.

Next day at lunchtime in school he even offered Ivan HIS dinner!

"That wee granny of yours frightened the living daylights out of me last night," he confessed. "I thought I was sent for! My whole nerves are away!"

As Ivan, and granny, both got older, feeding and clothing the growing boy became more of a problem.

Money was tight.

It was great when his father, or some other benevolent relative, bought him a new jersey or a new pair of shoes. Granny and he took whatever it was down to the pawn shop the next day, to obtain a few more shillings to eke out the pension.

The pawn shops were a lifeline to some people in that district. Young Ivan knew them well. Wilson's Pawn in Old Lodge Road and Tucker's Pawn in Agnes Street were granny's favourite trading places.

When he was twelve years old, Ivan took on a part-time job selling dulse for Maria Cush of Mateer Street.

Maria sold her dulse in threepenny bags. A good evening's work was to sell all thirty-six bags in your tomato-box. Of the nine shillings earned on the total sale, Maria, the Queen of the Dulse, got six shillings and the vendor kept the other three.

Ivan enjoyed this work. It took him up the Shankill Road and down the Falls Road. He used to call in all the public bars, for he knew that the more drunk his customers were, the more liberal they became.

"Here, son. There's a shilling. Give me four bags."

That was a good sale.

If he could give them a song, he could clear his box in any "pub". Ivan learnt that trick early on. So at the invitation of the customers he used to stand on a stool in the bars on the Falls Road and sing them a verse or two of a Loyalist song.

The revellers thought it was a huge joke, "Imagine a wee fella like you from the Shankill, singing for us on the Falls!" they would laugh.

Ivan didn't care what they said, or thought.

They bought his dulse, and that was all that mattered!

Then Ivan and his dulse-selling-mates had a brilliant idea. Or so they thought!

"What if we were to buy our own dulse and bag it ourselves? We could make far more money," they figured.

They put their enterprising plan into operation. Down to the markets they went, bought their own, bagged it and sold it. It meant more work but it also bought a more lucrative return.

The brighter the sunshine, the deeper the shadows, however! It also invoked the severe displeasure of Maria Cush! Who in one fell swoop had lost both her market and her sellers!

Ivan was making a little, a very little, money now.

Ivan was helping to support granny now.

But money couldn't solve the problem of which they were both become gradually more aware.

A maturing teenage boy and his elderly grandmother, living in the same room, both day and night, was beginning to prove increasingly difficult.

Something would have to be done.

And soon.

2

The Flit

In his early teens, and with a little money in his pocket, Ivan began to spend a lot of time out with his friends on the Shankill Road.

He didn't go a lot to school. Although granny packed him out every day he often found some more "interesting" activity to engage his youthful energy.

There were 'card-schools' in nearly every shop doorway. These 'schools' were comprised of small groups of young boys playing cards with hands that were almost too numb to hold anything, never mind deal cards. They huddled together for companionship. For something to while away the hours.

To prove that they weren't boys any more, Ivan and his mates began to smoke.

The money that he was making on the dulse, was tempting him to try and make more. By other 'easy', means. He learnt to visit the 'bookies' shops, to place bets on the horse-racing.

Granny used to reprimand him severely for staying out so late at nights. Ivan took little notice. Friday night, Saturday night and all day Sunday would be spent in pursuit of some sort of pleasure. It was an escape from the humdrum monotony of city-street-life.

One day in Mid-November 1962, Ivan was chatting to some of his friends in Belgrave Street, where granny and he were living at that particular time.

He was surprised, and perhaps just a little irritated, to hear his granny "calling him in", as she used to do when he was much younger. He reckoned himself to be a big boy now, and should be allowed to come and go at will.

But there was something about the excited urgency of her call that constrained him to disguise his displeasure.

"Ivan," she said, "could you come in a moment? I have something to tell you."

Having bidden his cronies a premature "Good night", Ivan followed his granny up into the upstairs room that served them as bedroom, kitchen, dining room and lounge.

When he closed the door behind him he found granny standing in the middle of the floor. She turned around to face him as he entered. Her hand held a brown envelope, but her expression told him nothing.

"Ivan, I've got a letter," she began.

He could see that much. Then his mind began to race. He thought of all the bicycles that he had removed from one location to another, for his convenience. 'Stolen' was not a word that he had used or liked. Then there was all that fruit which had mysteriously disappeared, little by little, from the pavement display outside Quinn's fruit shop on the Shankill Road.

A letter?!

"Is it a summons?" was the immediate response. Come to think of it, why else would she call him in from the street?

Granny's face creased into a smile. Then she gave a short laugh.

"No, it's not a summons," she reassured him. "It's from the Belfast Corporation. We have got a flat!"

The initial shock of it was too much for Ivan. He just stared at her, incredulously.

When he realised that it was true, that the nine years on the Corporation waiting list were over, he found his voice again.

"WE have got a flat!" he shouted

Then another thought struck him. There was something that he surely ought to find out.

"Where is it, granny?" he enquired, only slightly more subdued.

"It's in Hanna Street. Off York Street," granny answered.

Ivan had a fair idea where York Street was. But what did it matter?

"Great!" he exclaimed. "Great!"

Anywhere would be great after fourteen years of having being shifted about from one street to another, from one room to another and often in the middle of the night!

If granny had a disagreement with the landlord she would just announce, "Right, Ivan son, come on! We're going!"

And go they did, regardless of whatever time of the day, or night, it was!

Now all that would be over!

A flat of their own! Granny and Ivan! Marvellous!

Two weeks after they had received that very welcome letter, granny said to Ivan one afternoon, "I want you to go up to Mr. Yates in Urney Street, son, and hire a handcart. We are going to flit tomorrow."

Her teenage grandson was so looking forward to the move that he would have done anything possible to hasten it along. To hire a handcart would be no big problem.

They were going to a flat of their own!

Next morning, Ivan's uncle, his granny and himself carried their few pieces of simple furniture out of the rented room in Belgrave Street. Having placed all their bits and pieces, all their goods and chattels, on the handcart, they tied them down securely with ropes thrown over the top.

Granny then set off for Hanna Street in the trolley-bus. Ivan and his uncle were left to push the handcart to their new flat, on foot.

It was early December. Winter. A seeing-your-every-breath-in-front-of-you kind of day. Though they were well muffled up the fingers clutching the handles of the cart became locked-stiff and red-raw with the cold.

But Ivan didn't mind.

They were going to a flat of their own!

When uncle and Ivan arrived at their destination the darkness of the winter afternoon was beginning to cloak the city.

What an extremely pleasant reception awaited them!

Ivan's father had bought five bags of coal for granny and he. It had been delivered before their arrival.

Granny had a big roaring fire going. Their new living room was welcoming-warm. Light and bright. And best of all, their own!

After he entered the flat, Ivan instantly forgot about their belongings. They were still out in the street, still strapped to the handcart. His uncle could take care of them if he liked!

Granny and he did a conducted tour of their new abode. It was difficult to determine, who was conducting who. Granny wore a permanent satisfied smile which perfectly indicated the sense of satisfaction that she felt.

Ivan was just wildly excited. He ran, shouting, from one room to another. You couldn't shout in lodgings. The landlord would throw you out! But you could shout in YOUR OWN flat!

"A bath! Look at the bath, granny! You will have to get help when you get into that. Your daughter or somebody. You could drown in there, granny!"

Bertie Rice lived in the flat above. He and his wife had moved in a few months before.

His first reaction was one of amusement. "It must be all very new to them!" he said to his wife, with a knowing nod.

As the noise continued, his amusement turned to resignation.

"I wonder how long it will be till they settle down?" he asked.

However, as the frenzy below persisted his resignation gave way to an edginess.

"There must be about sixteen of them moved in down there!" he commented, almost fiercely. "Did you ever hear such a racket in your life? Yelling and bawling and banging doors. Where did the Corporation fall in with this crowd?"

Little did Bertie Rice know that at that moment there was not "a crowd" "down there". There weren't even "sixteen"!

There was Ivan, who was absolutely elated and extremely noisy.

There was granny, who was absolutely content, and extremely happy.

And there was uncle, who was absolutely exhausted and extremely frustrated.

He had just struggled in with most of the furniture!

But only granny and Ivan were to be Bertie's new neighbours.

Just the two of them!

Later on that evening the two new residents of Hanna Street were left alone. After he had been rested, warmed and fed, Ivan's uncle had left to return the by-now-much-lighter-handcart to Crimea Street.

There was so much to see, do and think about, that Ivan couldn't settle. He stood gazing out of the as-yet-curtainless windows at the carnival on the waste ground opposite. The noise, colour and movement of the coming-up-to-Christmas carnival held him spellbound.

When granny came into the living room from the hall, he was slightly startled.

"Here's something for you, Ivan," she said, quietly. "Hold out your hand."

Into her grandson's outstretched hand, granny pressed a key.

"That's the first front door key you have ever had, son," she remarked. "Now you can go out and enjoy yourself!"

Ivan was delighted.

He sat down before the fire in their solitary armchair and grasped his new key tightly in a clenched fist.

"Go out and enjoy yourself," she had said.

He would take her at her word!

He would give it a go.

3

A Tract Or A Sixpence

Ivan now had the key to their flat, which meant that he could come in when he pleased. And he enjoyed his absolute freedom.

After moving to Hanna Street he had attended Mountcollyer Secondary School for a year, but he had no interest whatsoever in things educational. All Ivan wanted to do was make money. Have money. Spend money.

So when he reached fifteen years of age he left school, to work in Rank's Flour Mill. He worked all the overtime he was offered, to earn as much money as he could.

Now that he was bringing home a regular wage, Ivan didn't forget granny. She had been good to him, and had made sacrifices for him, for fifteen years. Now it was his turn to be kind to her. He gave her a set weekly allowance.

The remainder of his wage every week, however, was spent on the habits which were by now an integral part of his life. He was smoking steadily, drinking frequently, and gambling on the cards and the horse-racing down to his very last sixpence, every week.

One decided advantage, for granny, of having "a place of her own", was that she could have visitors. You couldn't entertain visitors in lodgings, but you could have whoever you liked to visit you in your own flat.

Ivan's father, granny's son, had remarried and he and his new wife, Georgina, were regular visitors. They had an uncanny knack of turning up on a Saturday afternoon, just when Ivan was about to watch the three o'clock race from Sandown Park, on their state-of-the-art, rented, black and white money-in-the-slot TV!

Ivan's father is a sincere Christian, who was very active in local evangelical witness in those days.

So father and son didn't have a lot in common. They didn't see eye to eye, at all, on anything.

"Christians," Ivan would hiss scornfully, "Christians! They are no better than anybody else! The only difference between them and me is that they go to Church and I don't!

They sing hymns and I don't!

They read the Bible and I don't!

They cut their hair and I don't! ..."

Thus it went on.

Father would reply, presenting the gospel, simply.

Still Ivan mocked and argued.

In his estimation there was only one thing worse than wasting a whole Saturday afternoon wrangling about religion and that was having the TV go "F-I-Z-Z-Z-Z" ... in the middle of the Derby or the Grand National.

Then a real panic started. "Granny have you a two-bob-bit in your purse for the TV?" he would ask in desperation. If he hadn't one, and she hadn't one, then Ivan would dash up to the shop at the corner for change. Usually by the time he returned and put the two shilling piece in the slot, the race was over and there was a football match on!

That really used to leave him exasperated!

One of Ivan's father's reasons for visiting his mother and his son, was to have a bath! There were no baths in the houses on the Shankill Road, in the so-called "good old days", so for him it was a special privilege to have his mother living in a brand new modern flat! With a bath!

If he could only have his bath and keep quiet about it, that wouldn't be so bad, Ivan used to think. But he couldn't!

While Ivan was riveted to the television set, watching the racing to see how "his horse" was faring, father insisted on singing in the bath.

The strains of, "Jesus blood! Precious blood!" being sung lustily, came wafting into the living room. The accompaniment to father's Saturday solo was the musical splash of water around the bathroom.

Between races, Ivan used to look over at granny, and remark, with a wry smile, "You will have to spend the whole evening drying up the bathroom after that man, granny!"

As sure as his father sang hymns in the bath something unfortunate would happen to the horse that Ivan had backed. It either didn't start at all, or fell, or threw its rider, or took a wrong turning out on the course ...

But it never won!

After an occasional calamity Ivan would wink at granny and Georgina and say, "I can never win when he is in there!"

Pointing in the direction of the bathroom, he would pretend to whisper, "You see, he is praying in there, that my horse won't win!"

The two women would laugh and shake their heads, with Ivan doing his best to convince them, albeit light-heartedly.

The worst part of all was when father reappeared in the living room, blue towel wrapped around his head. Ivan's fallen horse was written all over Ivan's fallen face.

"Horse fall again, son! Isn't that a pity!" father would taunt, really rubbing it in. "More hard-earned money down the drain!"

Ivan used to shrug his shoulders and try to pass it off. He had another safety-valve. Music.

The mid-sixties saw the rapid rise to fame of The Beatles and The Rolling Stones. Ivan and his friends were fervent fans of these popular beat groups.

Following such famous pop-stars wasn't even enough in itself for these teenage admirers. They went a step further.

From enthusiastic admiration they progressed to attempted emulation.They formed their own group, called the Crazy Beats. Ivan was the lead singer.

In keeping with the beat-scene of that generation, they wore casual shirts, grew their hair to their shoulders and made lots and lots of noise!

The bigger the racket they could raise, the better they thought they were!

One Saturday afternoon, Ivan was in the final stages of preparing to go out. His friends were waiting for him, jammed like sardines into the tiny entrance hall.

Dad's bath was over and he was watching idly as his seventeen-year-old son tilted his head first to one side, then to the other, before the mirror. He was combing down his shoulder-length hair. It had to be just right.

They had been talking about the gospel and Christian things. Ivan's father had long-since acquired the ability to steer any conversation on to a "spiritual matters" track.

"You see Christians!" pronounced Ivan, with a flamboyant wave of his comb, "Pack of hypocrites the whole lot of them!"

When his father didn't reply, Ivan continued with gusto, "I know one around the corner there. Salvation Army man he is. He sends the children messages. And do you know what he gives them? A tract. A TRACT!

You see my old granny there. She sends the children messages, too. Do you know what she gives them? A sixpence!"

Ivan was well wound up now. As much to impress his waiting pals, as to convince his unusually unresponsive father, he went on, "That's Christians for you. They will give you sermons! They will give you talks! They will give you tracts! They will give you anything, only a bob!"

By the time Ivan had finished this last tirade, Dad had hung his head, away down low.

"I suppose you could be right," he responded, at length, meekly.

It appeared like a victory for his forceful son. But it was hollow, shallow, sour.

Ivan felt miserable.

"Now you have hurt your da," he said to himself.

He had to make instant amends. It would be impossible to relax and enjoy himself, singing with the Crazy Beats, troubled by a nagging guilty conscience.

"It's not YOU I'm talking about, da. You know that!" he explained hastily, intending to set both of their minds at rest. "I don't mean you, personally. I'm talking about all those other chancers running about the streets out there!"

"Well, really Ivan I'm sure I must be much the same as the rest of them. How can I be any different?" Father was continuing to play the chastened child.

Then he lifted his head.

Suddenly changing his tone of voice, he switched from defence to attack. "You seem to know how the Christian life should be lived," father observed.

Ivan was consoled. The hurt didn't appear to have gone too deep.

"Don't worry, da," he declared, confidently, "I know the difference between the genuine article and the fakes. No problem. I can spot a phoney a mile away."

Little did Ivan know but his father had been manoeuvring him very cleverly into a position where he could hit him with a verbal knockout punch.

"Well, then, why don't YOU get saved and show them how the Christian life should really be lived? You seem to know far more about it than anybody else," he retorted.

Ivan said no more. There was no answer to that.

He had caught himself in his own snare. It would be stupid to pull the noose any tighter.

Turning his back on his father, his granny and Georgina, he mumbled, "Cheerio everybody," back over his shoulder. With that he strode out into the hall, to where his friends were still patiently waiting.

"Come on, fellas, let's go!" he uttered, tersely.

As they streamed out into the street, one of the group, a Crazy Beat, asked him, "Hey, what was all that about in there?"

Gradually Ivan slowed his pace to a saunter. He had his coat slung over his shoulder in an attempt to appear casual. His offhand attitude was a subconscious over-reaction to disguise a hollow-hole inside him.

"Oh, my father just informed me that it doesn't cost anything to be a critic!" he remarked, almost flippantly.

A lesson had been learnt.

With those Beatle-mania years came a very slow, but equally very steady increase in popularity for the Crazy Beats on the music scene. They were never going to make the really big time, but they had their own local recognition-zone in north Belfast. Their favourite venue was a small hall above a public house in North Queen Street.

Something better than being popular in their own peculiar patch was having their own little fan club. And the big bonus was that their fan club members, who followed them to most of the dances where they played, were ninety per cent female!

Girls!

The Crazy Beat musicians revelled in the adulation of these teenage followers. There was a small nucleus of these loyal young supporters who followed them everywhere and that even included to their practice sessions.

One of these I'll-go-where-you-go fans was a girl called Sylvia.

Ivan had noticed her particularly from her very first attendance at a Crazy Beat session. Sylvia was a petite red-head, and still a teenage schoolgirl at Mount Vernon.

Initially, she had come to hear the Crazy Beats and dance to their music, because she was a cousin of the lead guitarist.

Now she was hooked! She liked these guys, and their music. In that order.

It was Sylvia's dancing that Ivan spotted first. She was a marvellous dancer, lithe, enthusiastic and never seemed to tire.

Standing with the group, singing away, Ivan would gaze at her. He watched her movements. He admired her supple skill. As the heat built up in the hall as the evening progressed, Sylvia's face began to glow and her eyes seemed to sparkle.

That made her all the more attractive to him. So Ivan just watched her more intently!

BUT NO! Ivan hadn't time for girls.

He had the music.

He had the bookies.

He had the card-schools.

These were all so important to him. They demanded most of his leisure time, and all of his spending money.

Ivan couldn't spare the time to get involved with anybody. He hadn't time to think seriously about Sylvia.

At least, not yet!

4

"SNAP!"

The Crazy Beat group played in the bars and halls of north Belfast for almost two years, with their ever faithful fan club following them to every dance.

As the months passed, and she was always there, Ivan found it increasingly difficult to disguise his admiration for Sylvia. Then he became aware of something that pleased him. The feeling seemed to be mutual. She was showing definite signs of interest in him. Ivan reckoned that she was coming to every dance for more than the dancing now. Sylvia was coming to see him!

Their conversations before and after Ivan sang were becoming longer, and more enjoyable. It didn't take the Crazy Beat group members or the rest of their loyal supporters very long to sense that there was something special about the friendship between Ivan and Sylvia. It was soon to become an accepted fact amongst them that Ivan and Sylvia were "going out with each other".

They walked the streets of Belfast together, chatting and relishing each other's company. Occasionally they "went up to the pictures". If money was scarce but the night was wet, they went to "The Duncairn", in Duncairn Gardens, but if they were feeling flush some evening and the film was supposed-to-be-super they went to "The Capital" on the Antrim Road. The Capital was a more expensive, "up-market" cinema at that time.

Having more and more money to spend was becoming an obsession with Ivan. He changed his job several times, always hoping for "big money" quickly. He needed lots of money to maintain his life style. Where was he going to find it?

He started to gamble heavily. If only I could make a series of winning bets, Ivan used to think, then I would have nothing to worry about. Life would surely be easy from then on.

So he went to the dogs. Literally. There was greyhound racing in Dumore Stadium every Tuesday, Thursday and Saturday evening, and in Celtic Park every Monday, Wednesday and Friday. That meant he could bet on six nights of the week if he wanted to. And he did want to! It became a craving with him. Every night that he wasn't out with Sylvia he was at "the sixty-minute cleaners" as he and his buddies used to call them. They figured that it only took them an hour "to clean you "! And sometimes even less! Yet still they went on every available night of the week.

This night or that night was always going to be THE night. The night of the big win!

One foggy-cum-rainy November night Ivan and a friend were at Celtic Park. The atmosphere was electric. The floodlights were glaring, the loudspeakers were blaring, and the bets were pouring in. Then suddenly the heavens opened. The rain came down in sheets, the track was soon awash and everybody huddled around the course absolutely soaked.

There was just one race left so it was going to be run, when the track was cleared. Ivan and his friend had half-a-crown left between them.

His mate was tipsy and totally oblivious to rain or discomfort or anything else. He said to Ivan, "I have a feeling about number six. We will put our last half-crown on it."

The only feelings that Ivan had were the rain trickling down the back of his neck, the trousers stuck tightly to his soaking legs, and his feet squelching in his shoes. He was past caring about number six, or number two, or number whatever ... He just wanted out of there.

"No. Save that last half-crown and we will take the bus home," he replied.

"I know a winner when I see one!" his friend asserted positively. "I'm putting this half-crown on him!"

He did.

Number six was sixth out of six! Last!

Ten minutes later, as they were walking through the gates of the stadium, to start the long trudge home, bus money betted away, a taxi passed them. Ivan stared in amazement!

Peering out of the steamed up back window was a greyhound!

Grabbing his friend by the arm, Ivan pointed with the other hand, "Would you look at that!" he yelled. "We have to slog home in the bucketing rain, and the greyhounds are going home in taxis!"

He was beginning to see the emptiness of it all. Yet it didn't stop him.

Ivan was a regular customer in the "bookies". Greyhound racing was in the evenings. Horse racing was for the afternoons.

One crowded Saturday afternoon in the local turf accountants, Ivan had just placed his bet and was standing having a smoke with a friend. They were waiting for the results to come in, as were dozens of others.

All of a sudden, the chap that he was standing with asked him, "Did you ever notice, Ivan, that this place has five hatches to take your money in, and only one to pay you out?"

It was right. When he looked across at the hatches, Ivan became instantly aware of something which had never registered with him before. There WERE five windows with steady trickling queues at them. Then there was another hatch, removed a short distance from the others. That was where they paid you out when you had won.

There was nobody at it.

Ivan stood dumbfounded for a moment, contemplating the significance of this realisation. His friend knew that he had given Ivan an unexpected shock - like touching an electric fence without knowing what it is.

So he pressed home his point. "And I hear that the owner of this place is going to the Bahamas again for his holidays this year," he continued. "And see you and me, we will be lucky if we make it to the City Hall, if the weather's good!"

The futility of the betting game was beginning to hit home. First the greyhounds, and now the bookies. Both were a waste of time and money. Something stirred within him, warning him that he must be some kind of a fool.

But STILL it didn't stop him!

What else was there to do? One of these days he was going to make his fortune! Hit the big bet! Then it would all come good. He would go on some spree!

The long awaited 'big bet' didn't materialise, however. Days became more and more monotonous and mundane.

Sylvia was the only glimmer of light in the ever-gathering gloom. Ivan enjoyed their nights out together, but he needed money to buy her things and take her places. He was dead keen to impress!

So he turned to crime. He justified it to himself by calling it "robbing the rich to pay the poor."

"The rich," were residents of the Upper Cavehill Road or the Malone Road. Occasionally he would decide to get "a breath of sea air" and extend his attentions to the seaside-rich in Helen's Bay or Craigavad. There were plentiful pickings in suburbia. And there was a disgusting imbalance in the world!

Ivan reasoned that if people had two cars in the drive and a garden as big as a field they could easily spare a pound or two to help "the poor".

Him!

Having given it some thought, he devised his own method of "working" as he described it. Always alone Ivan would approach a house which he had been staking out for a few days. It would usually be a house with more than one car, well dressed adults, and children with smart school uniforms, violin cases and ponies in the paddock.

On a day when the children were at school and there were no cars in the drive, Ivan would approach the back door. If there was no response to an initial knock, and the door was unlocked, he would push it open gently, still knocking repeatedly and calling, "Hello, hello, anyone at home?

When he found somebody at home he would say, "Oh, hello, Missus. I am starting a wee window cleaning business in the area. I was wondering if you would be interested in having your windows cleaned every week or fortnight or so?"

If Missus was interested in having her windows cleaned, her name was entered in Ivan's little black book, which he always carried with him. It was important to appear business-like! If she wasn't interested he just told her how sorry he was, and left.

On the other hand, however, if there was NOBOBY around, Ivan used to scan the kitchen hastily, but thoroughly, for purses, rings, watches ... anything that was small, valuable and easily concealed. With a deft and lightning touch he would then fill his pockets, and make a controlled exit!

He began to enjoy this life of petty crime.

More than the greyhounds were travelling by taxi now! It was taxis and trains and a nice suit of clothes. The life style suited him. It was something he had often dreamt about.

For a strange reason he used to love wet Monday afternoons. It afforded Ivan a queer sardonic satisfaction to wind down a taxi window and wave with unwarranted enthusiasm to the workers coming plodding o ut of Rank's Flour Mill, in groups of two or three. Their heads would be bowed against the persistent drizzle, and the flour would soon become caked on their overalls with the wet.

"Keep it up lads! You're doing a good job!" he would call out, taunting them.

For almost nine months Ivan lived a very pleasant easy life. He wanted to share his newly-acquired affluence with the two people whom he cared most cared about, granny and Sylvia, but he had to be careful. So he slipped granny the occasional fiver, and bought Syliva a surprise present now and again. Not enough to arouse any suspicions, but just enough to keep the pair of them happy!

When he was engaged in his sporadic thieving, Ivan never stopped to consider the consequences. It couldn't last. Not forever. Some day, some way, he was sure to be found out!

One summer evening in 1967 he was standing alone at a bus stop on the Somerton Road in Belfast. He had two rings, a watch and a substantial amount of money in his pocket, all of which he had only just "acquired".

It was a balmy evening and as he was waiting for the bus to come he pondered idly what he would do with the loot. He had to be careful with disposal too!

Glancing up the road he noticed that a police van was coming down. "The doggie wagon" he and his mates used to call it. Never mind, he would just stand innocently at the bus stop and they would drive on past about their business.

But they didn't!

The van began to slow down as it approached him.

As it drew to a halt before him, Ivan noticed that the constable looking out of the van window had a big round red face. Like a moon.

He thought, "Now there's a countryman if ever I saw one."

Ivan's "countryman" was a man of few words. Winding down the window he glared at Ivan and growled through clenched teeth, "Get in!"

"Oh, are you giving me a lift?" Ivan replied, trying to appear totally unconcerned. "That's really civil of you, officer."

Constable Redface didn't even bother to look as Ivan clambered into he back of the van. Staring fixedly forward he continued gruffly, "Yes. You are getting a lift O.K. To Glenravel Street barracks. We have been looking for you for months."

Dusting down his precious suit, Ivan replied, "Well now, that's odd. I have been living with my granny down in York Street. If you had wanted to come down and see us you would have been very welcome any time." He was trying to keep up a rapidly-thinning veneer of jauntiness. "I'm not up round these houses all the time. I just came up here for a bit of a stroll this evening."

There was no answer. Just stony silence.

Obviously they hadn't heard him over the noise of the engine. Or perhaps they weren't convinced.

It was useless trying to talk to them. He gave up and spoke to another "passenger" instead.

On arrival at Glenravel Street Police Station, Ivan was shown into an interview room by himself. The constables who had brought him in, left him there, and two detectives took over.

"Empty your pockets!" was the first demand from one of them

When all the spoils were spread out on the table the questions came in rapid succession.

"Where did you get those rings?"

"Where did you get that watch?"

"Where did you get all that money from?" ...

It was going to be difficult to explain all this away.

"Well, the rings belong to my girlfriend," Ivan began, "I found the watch and I got a bet up on the horses."

When he had finished he realised that his excuses were altogether too lame. The detectives just smirked and gave knowing nods. They were not impressed.

It hadn't even dawned on Ivan yet that if these items hadn't been reported missing already, they certainly would be within the next couple of days.

"Would you have any objections to having your finger prints taken?" the by-now very suspicious sergeant enquired.

"Not at all," was the cheery reply. "Happy to oblige. You've got an innocent man here. There must be some mistake. But I have nothing to hide."

"Here then, lend us your hand a minute," was the next request.

The hand that was outstretched to receive its first key-of-the-flat was now held out to have finger prints taken. When the tips of his fingers had been dipped into the ink, the sergeant pressed them, finger-by-finger onto a sheet of paper.

After he had handed Ivan a rag on which to clean his hand, the sergeant made off, out of the room, with the sheet of printed paper. As he was slowly and methodically wiping his ink-stained fingers, a constable came in with a cup of tea for Ivan.

"Can't be too bad a place this," he mused. "And they must be fairly decent chaps, bringing me tea and all. I will probably be out of here within the hour."

He had only just finished his welcome cup of tea when the sergeant burst back into the room, carrying two sheets of paper. He had one in each hand and a beaming smile on his face.

It was a long time since Ivan had seen anybody looking so extremely pleased with himself.

"Snap!" he shouted, almost triumphantly.

"That's strange," Ivan replied, subdued.

"Do you know what is even more strange?" the officer continued with a laugh. "We have found these prints in half the houses in Belfast!"

5

The Missing Piece

The magistrate looked down sternly over his half-frame spectacles. He had his eyes half-closed, like a child trying to peer squinty-eyed down the neck of a milk bottle. Having listened to the charges being read out, he pronounced sentence. "You are a menace to society. I am going to send you to prison. It will help you."

Ivan's heart sank. "Thanks," he replied, unable to veil a bitter sarcasm.

He was then led down to the cells below the court. It was a chilling ordeal. He cheered up marginally though when he met two of his former chums down there. These men were older, and more experienced in such matters.

Bottled up within Ivan there was a strange mixture of apprehension, fear, uncertainty and excitement. All these feelings were churning around inside him, but none was predominant. He had never felt anything like this before, for he didn't know what was ahead of him. He had absolutely no idea what to expect.

Trying to calm himself down, he thought he would speak to these old mates about it, if he got the chance. They would know. They had been "inside" already, many times.

When he had pushed up beside them, as close as he dared without arousing suspicion, he whispered, "Tell me, boys, what is it like? 'The big house' I mean." Ivan was trying to be smart, establish himself as "one of the lads", by calling Crumlin Road Prison by its hardly-affectionate nickname.

Looking furtively from side to side, like a lion guarding its prey, one of them snarled a single word out of the corner of his mouth.

He said, "Butlins!"

Ivan was amazed. "Ach, away!" he replied in disbelief. That had never been his image of the foreboding building, when he had passed it on the bus on the Crumlin Road.

His friends went on to recount all the former acquaintances and accomplices who were in the prison.

"Do you know So and so? ... Well he's up there," they said.

"And you will remember What's his name? He's up there as well," they said.

So it went on.

By the time they had completed their curt recollections, Ivan was actually looking forward to "going up".

As with so many things in life, however, the realisation did not live up to the expectation.

Prison was not Butlins.

It was a regime of rules, regulations and routine. None of these things Ivan had ever been used to. There were no "wee danders" at midnight now, when he felt like it! There was no basic freedom!

This was captivity. This was isolation from all that he had valued, from everything that had been "life" for him.

There were no greyhounds here. No bookies. No Crazy Beats. No granny. And worst and loneliest of all, no Sylvia.

Now he had time to think. Time to think about others, as well as himself.

Throughout all his escapades, his arrest, his trial and his sentence, he had only been concerned with one person. That was Number One. Ivan Thompson, himself, alone. There never had been any thought for anyone else.

Not father. Not granny. Not Sylvia.

And certainly not God.

Now he had time. Lots and lots of time to reflect. He wasn't going to be travelling any farther than the wood-shed where he sawed logs, any day. Then back to his cell for "lock up". That was when it hit him.

In those late-night lonely sessions he would leaf through the Gideon Bible which had been placed in his cell. When he discovered the reference section at the front he used to scan the titles.

"What to read when you are lonely," it said.

"I'm lonely," thought Ivan. "I must read that." The Bible was a totally alien book to him. He didn't know how to find the place in it. He learnt slowly, and by trial and error. There was little else to do, and he had plenty of spare time. Syliva wouldn't be on the phone, and the Crazy Beats wouldn't be up at the door.

"What to read when you are depressed," it said.

"I'm depressed," thought Ivan. "Who wouldn't be in a place like this? I must read that."

So it was that Ivan had his first serious, continuous contact with the Word of God, in prison.

Autumn gave way to winter. Days became shorter and the nights much longer. It was bitterly cold in the wood-yard. You had to saw harder for longer, just to keep warm.

With winter came Christmas. Ivan hated the thought of it. For some of his fellow-prisoners Crumlin Road might have been Butlins, but not for him. They had nobody else to care for them, but he had. They had nobody else that they cared about, but he had.

He was seriously missing Sylvia. He thought often of his lonely but loyal granny. He had disgraced his father.

Christmas, the season of love and joy, peace and friendship, was going to be a sad and solitary experience for him.

The only transient relief from the hum-drum monotony of the wood-sawing days, were the leisure times. A number of prisoners were allowed to mix for an hour each day to play minor games, throw darts or watch TV. They were especially fond of escape movies!

Ivan liked the darts. He had played a few times before in pubs, but now his game was improving with practice. He was acquiring both the skill and the slang. Scoring a "double top" was becoming a more frequent occurrence.

One evening, when he was in the middle of a game with two others, he heard a grunt behind him.

On turning around, Ivan became aware of a huge frame standing beside him, totally dominating the corner where they were playing. He had often observed this mountain of a man, with the thick bull-neck and the mighty muscles, from a distance. Nobody ever went too close to him if they could possibly help it. He was in prison for violence. Grievous bodily harm was stamped all over his massive bulk and scowling expression.

"I've got this jig-saw puzzle. My brother sent it in. I will need a hand to do it," he snarled. "You will help me with it, Ivan."

There was no "Will you?" or "Would you like to?" or "You don't mind me asking but I was wondering if ...?"

No questions were asked. No volunteers were requested.

It was quite simply, "You will help me with it, Ivan."

Knowing that he must comply, but unwilling to undertake any project alone with the awesome presence, he offered the services of his two friends as well.

"Oh yes, I'll help you," Ivan responded cheerily, "and so will my two mates here. Won't you lads?"

They all agreed to help, thinking, "Jigsaw puzzle. No problem. Half-an-hour will do it."

It looked so ridiculous. There was a giant of a man striding across the leisure room clutching a small cardboard jig-saw puzzle box in a hand that was designed for a sledgehammer. Following him closely, like trained-to-heel gundogs, were Ivan and his two ex-darts playing cronies.

They were having mixed feelings about it. An interest had been stirred within them. A jig-saw puzzle would be something different to do, a pleasant diversion. None of them had seen once since they were young boys. The overriding feeling, however, was one of fear.

It would be patently unwise to refuse!

On reaching a table that pleased him, jig-saw-jumbo opened his box and unceremoniously tipped out its contents.

Ivan's heart sank.

It was a one-thousand piece puzzle. The table top was covered with tiny pieces, and many of them seemed to be exactly the same, either blue or a rich golden colour. There must be a lot of sky or straw in this picture!

How were they ever going to make head or tail of it?

"Right boys. Let's get started!" the boss-man growled.

So they all got started.

Three of them around the table were trying to fix the pieces gently together, but the king-of-the-puzzle was banging them into position with his huge fist.

Ivan leaned over. "Hey, mate, you don't need to hammer the pieces like that!"

Immediately after he had spoken, he realised that he had made a mistake. The words had floated off into the air. They couldn't be recalled.

The clenched fist hovered in mid-air. "Oh, do you not!" was the roared response. "Well, that's the way I do it! O.K.?"

Then, by way of emphasis, the suspended fist descended on the table with a tremendous crash.

"O.K!" said Ivan, "O.K!" He decided that it would be best not to contradict this master-puzzler. His friends and he concluded that if thumping was what the pieces needed, then thumping was what the pieces would get. So they all joined in.

It sounded like drums. Bang! Bang! Bang! on the table, bashing tiny cardboard pieces into place.

After the first evening there were small groups of joined up pieces which weren't ready to be joined up to anything else, scattered all over the table. There were also hundreds of single unattached pieces tipped back into the lid of the box.

When leisure time was over, and they were called to return to their cells, the boss-man looked from one to another around his three assistants, purposefully.

"I'll see you all back here again tomorrow evening," he announced. "Sure there's none of you planning to go anywhere?"

Obviously tomorrow evening's leisure time was to be spent in jig-saw puzzling as well.

It was.

So also was the next evening, and the next, and the next ....

Ivan and his friends surprised themselves when they each had to admit individually, but inwardly, that they were actually beginning to enjoy it. Their pleasure and anticipation increased as the rural landscape with its foreground duckpond, hay shed with bales of hay protruding and distant hills silhouetted against a cloudless sky, unfolded.

Having devoted every leisure period for almost two weeks to their task, the four persistent puzzle-bashers were nearing the climax of their efforts.

There were only four pieces left on the table. Glancing from them across to the virtually completed puzzle, Ivan was gripped by a sense of disappointment which rapidly turned to horror.

What had happened? Or what was going to happen now?

There were still five spaces left in the puzzle. Four into five wouldn't fit!

The mighty man who had instigated the jig-saw puzzling evenings, had made it clear all along that he wanted to be the one to finish the puzzle. He was going to hammer home the last piece!

Ivan sensed that there was going to be a problem. A big problem!

There wasn't going to be a final piece!

When the resolute fist had firmly fixed the last available bit into position, there was one space left, relatively tiny, but somehow glaringly obvious. It was right in the middle of the hay shed!

The big man's eyes scoured the table. Like a radar scanner, back and forward, back and forward ...

After a momentary hush, a bellow went up.

"There's a piece missing!"

Ivan knew that there would be a row. There just had to be! Glowering over at him, the chief-puzzle-maker shouted, "Ivan, where's the missing bit?"

Not knowing where it was, Ivan turned to the lad on his left. Putting his arm around his shoulder he said, jokingly, "Give him back that missing piece or we are all for it!"

"I haven't got it!" he yelled in fright.

The chap at the far end of the table, the youngest, had turned ashen-pale and was shaking in his seat. They were all intimidated by their self-appointed leisure leader.

"My brother sent me in that puzzle," he complained. The bawling had subsided to a growling and scowling. "He probably knew that there was apiece missing and sent it in to me for badness. I will do for him the next time he dares to come to see me! I will screw the little neck off him!"

With that he rose, and grabbing the table with both hands, upended it. The whole puzzle disintegrated as it slid to the floor, ending up in a neat heap of pieces. Some of them remained interlocked and were sticking out at crazy angles.

As he gazed at the pile of coloured cardboard, Ivan thought of one of those factory chimneys that had just been blown up, lying in a pile of smoking rubble.

He and his two companions stared in dismay at the end result of their fortnight's effort. At least they were all thankful for one thing. They hadn't had their "little necks screwed off"!

The roaring continued.

Mayhem ensued.

"Everybody back to their cells!" the warders called above the din.

Normally the prisoners would be reluctant to return to their cells. Not this time! The three assistant puzzle-makers were glad to make a hasty retreat to isolation and safety.

Sitting on his bed, a few minutes later, Ivan heard the disillusioned King of the Puzzle being escorted back to his cell, still snarling out threats to his luckless brother!

In an easy flowing movement he turned up his plimsoll to unlace it, before taking it off. As he caught a fleeting glimpse of the sole of his slipper, he was forced to look again. There was something stuck to it.

Almost fearfully Ivan picked the object from his sole. Could it be? Could it possibly be what he feared it was?

Yes! It was the missing piece!

He was gripped by a sinking sickening sensation.

What was he going to do with it?

He couldn't hide it in his cell. A warder would find it.

He definitely couldn't throw it out through the window into the exercise yard. He had a sudden horrible vision of somebody shouting, "Hi, look what I've found! Isn't that the missing puzzle piece?"

No. That wasn't a possibility either.

As the sense of fear and panic increased Ivan decided that there was only one course of action open to him. It was drastic, but instinctive.

Slipping the misplaced piece into his mouth he began to chew up the cardboard. After having chewed for a few moments the piece of puzzle became a mass of pulp.

Then he swallowed it.

Ivan ate the missing piece!

Still he was terrified. Life for him could have very unpleasant undertones if the mighty man ever found out about his puzzle-piece performance.

"His little neck" was still on the danger list. It could be "screwed off" yet!

His release couldn't come too soon!

6

Released Into Captivity

"It was a pleasure to meet you, lads. We will probably see you all again sometime. It likely won't be long until you are back!"

The prison warder was exchanging light-hearted banter with each of the men as he opened the small outer door to release them, one by one, out on to the Crumlin Road. Ivan was one of six men who had completed their sentences, and were released together that day.

It was a bright Spring morning, and marvellous to be free.

Ivan and the other five men waited for each other and gradually formed a dazed cluster at the outside door. It was wonderful just to see and hear the Corporation buses moving up and down the road. There were a few people who rode past on bicycles. Ivan had his memory jarred. He had almost forgotten what a bike looked like. Then there were the people. Two women carrying home shopping bags of groceries were talking noisily to each other. A woman was wheeling a pram with another child toddling along beside it, holding on. There was an old arthritic man walking an old arthritic dog.

The amazing thing about it was that they were free, all free, to come and go as they pleased!

When the group on the footpath was six-strong and acclimatising to freedom, they agreed that there was only one thing that they wanted to do. They just had to go for a drink. It had been a long dry winter. They had all been handed some money before leaving so they had to find a public bar!

Therein lay a problem. Religion had never been an issue inside the prison. Now they were out, liberated into society. When they began to exercise their freedom of choice the distinctive divisions in Belfast society became evident, even in 1967.

"What about the Greyhound Bar on the Shankill Road?" Ivan suggested.

Two of the six were Roman Catholics.

"No way!" one of them retorted, "I wouldn't be seen dead in it! What about Brennan's Bar on the Falls?"

"Some of us would be dead if we went into it," was Ivan's reply.

There was a thoughtful silence. Had they reached an immediate impasse? Surely their much-talked-about and long-awaited plans to "get full" weren't going to founder on the rock of religious divide?

Eventually one of the chaps had a bright idea. "Let's go down to Ann Street in the city centre," he proposed. "I know where there is a good wee pub down there, and it will be neutral ground for all of us."

Everyone agreed readily to that proposition. It seemed an obvious solution to what could have been an awkward situation.

The group then set off, chatting together, down the Crumlin Road towards the oasis. They weren't in any hurry as they savoured life "outside". Slowly and steadily they were familiarising themselves with scents, sounds and scenes which they thought they had forgotten.

In the midst of the babble of their conversation, Ivan noticed, out of the corner of his eye, a little grey head coming bobbing up the footpath. Below the little grey head was a tiny frail body.

It was granny.

She had been running. She had been planning for months to be at the door to welcome her wayward grandson on his release.

A lump rose in Ivan's throat. His mouth dried up and his interest in his would-be drinking partners and their shallow chatter, evaporated. A sentimental weakness, fuelled by half-a -lifetime's love and respect, overcame him.

Drinking was unimportant now.

"You can drink my share of the money, boys!" he said, impulsively. "I'm away."

With that he started to run down the footpath to meet her, arms outstretched.

On hearing the pounding of his footsteps on the pavement granny looked up. When she saw Ivan bearing down towards her at full throttle she started to run again, exhausted though she was. She too had her arms open wide. Big tears were trickling down over her protruding cheek-bones.

In one flowing, sweeping movement Ivan lifted his little granny off the ground. Like a child lifting a highly-prized doll and holding it up for all to see, he hoisted her as high as he could. The tiny frame hung suspended in mid-air, her black skirts fluttering in the stiff Spring breeze.

"Oh granny I have hurt you! I have disgraced you! But you have been so good to me! How have you been bothered with me for all these years?" Words of appreciation and apology just tumbled from his lips. They were the spontaneous outpouring of a stricken conscience.

Granny was great. She had been so loyal, but she was also extremely shy.

"Put me down! Put me down for goodness sake!" she cried in excited embarrassment. "Can you not see that all the people are looking at us?"

Ivan was not even remotely concerned about who was looking at them. It didn't matter to him. He had spent a lonely winter in prison and this little women had visited him faithfully every week.

At long last, after having spun her around a few times, and having given her one final shake until her teeth rattled and her wispy grey hair sat out at right angles to her head, he did set her down like a delicate doll, on the pavement.

"Oh Ivan, you are a terrible fellow!" granny exclaimed. She didn't mean a word of it though!

The few mildly amused spectators reluctantly drifted back to whatever it was they had been doing.

The show was over.

Six men had agreed to go for a drink in a 'good wee pub' in Ann Street.

One had met his granny.

Now there were five.

Chuckling together they set off ahead of the reunited pair. Prison had been too much for their mate, they concluded. He had gone soft.

Totally oblivious to where they were, or what others thought, Ivan and granny started on the walk back to the flat in Hanna Street. As they walked, they talked. It was marvellous to be able to speak to each other freely again.

In the course of that emotional conversation, Ivan was to learn just how much this caring little granny had been planning for him, even when he had been out from under her roof.

"I've saved a pound or two out of my pension to buy you a new suit," she said in a matter-of-fact fashion.

After some discussion on the colour of the coming new outfit, she continued with, "And I have an interview for a job lined up for you, as well."

As all the details of her private planning during that difficult winter became revealed, little by little, Ivan knew that it had all cost her much in time and energy, and in skimping and doing without.

He made a resolution there and then.

Granny talked on eagerly, and as she talked Ivan responded, but only mechanically. At the thinking-behind-talking level he was wrestling with a renewed determination to sort himself out.

"Here is a wee woman whose whole life revolves around me, and I am an absolute waster," he reasoned. "I will have to try and repay her for all her kindness. Somehow, some way, soon. She's getting on."

On returning to the flat and easing back into normal life, Ivan made a sincere attempt to put his resolution into practice. Granny's job prospect materialised and he was soon earning again.

He began by giving her little treats that she appreciated.

There were the occasional boxes of sweets, bunches of flowers and days out to Bangor. Any luxury, however small, was more than granny had ever been used to, and how she used to thank him profusely!

As the weeks passed, and with unlimited freedom in his movement and spending money in his pocket there returned to Ivan's door and his life those friends and habits of previous years.

There was a new suit on the man. Granny had seen to that.

But there wasn't a new man in the suit, and granny could do nothing about that.

The desire for a flutter on the greyhounds was still there. Nights out with the boys in the pub were becoming frequent again. Card 'schools' in the flat until two o'clock in the morning were commonplace once more.

The shackles of bondage were beginning to tighten around him again. They were strangling his soul be degrees.

Gradually granny's treats became fewer, but she didn't complain. She saw it coming. Ivan was spending more and more money on purely personal pleasure.

Prison had removed the menace from society but it hadn't removed the monster of selfish sin from his life.

7

Wedding And Weeping

Although the prison winter had been a difficult one for both of them, the love link between Ivan and Sylvia hadn't died. If anything it had become stronger.

Sylvia had visited Ivan as often as she possibly could. Sometimes she came alone, sometimes with granny. Their common love and concern for Ivan had drawn the two women closer together. A bond was developing between them. Indeed there were some nights that Sylvia stayed overnight with granny to help relieve the loneliness.

Six months after his release, Ivan and Sylvia were out for a walk. It was August 1968, and a beautiful summer evening. As they strolled up Duncairn Gardens, in north Belfast, the sun shone brightly, the leaves rustled on the trees, and lightly-clad children were darting about as they played their games on the pavements.

With the sun on his back, and Sylvia on his arm, Ivan felt happy and relaxed. He knew that he wasn't going to get a better girl than this. There certainly wouldn't be anyone fonder of him than Sylvia was.

He decided the time was ripe to put to her an idea that he had been toying with for some time.

"If things would work out, Sylvia, I think you and me should get married," was how he phrased it. When Sylvia glanced round into his face, with a pleased but puzzled expression, he began to realise what that simple statement meant to her.

As she didn't respond instantly, Ivan was granted the opportunity of qualifying his proposal with one condition. There was a problem which had been with him for some time - it had probably stopped him from "popping the question" earlier. It was the "how can I handle two women in my life? dilemma. "If I marry Sylvia, what will I do with granny?" was his predicament.

Ivan knew that during his imprisonment Sylvia and granny had become much closer. This encouraged him.

"There's just one wee thing about it though, Sylvia," he went on, kicking a stone off the pavement, into the middle of the road. "I'm worried about granny. I would never want her to be lonely, as she has been so good to me. Could we get married and move in with her until she dies, or at least get a wee house near her and keep her company? She will soon be needing a lot of attention."

His last statement was his first expression to anyone of a growing concern. He had noticed that granny was slowing up. She wasn't as able physically, or as alert mentally, as she used to be.

By the time Ivan had finished, Sylvia was ready to respond to Ivan's proposal with its inbuilt, but hardly difficult and certainly understandable, condition. Neither marrying Ivan or attending granny seemed to pose any problem for her. After all, she loved them both by now.

"Oh, granny would be no trouble. That would be O.K. Don't worry about her," Sylvia replied reassuringly. "When were you thinking about for the wedding? This year or next year?"

Ivan was struck dumb. Time for more quick thinking. He studied the dark mass of the Cavehill with more interest than it deserved. The sun had gone from it now, leaving it silhouetted against a pale orange sky.

"Hardly this year anyway he reasoned with himself. It's August now. What will I tell her?"

Having never given the finer details of a wedding even the slightest moment's consideration, Ivan had to put on a good show to sound convincing.

"Oh next year, sometime," he said, at length, trying to appear as though he had been contemplating the matter for months.

Sylvia wasn't to be palmed off with a generalisation like that. She had further questions.

"What month next year?" she wanted to know.

Playing for thinking time again, Ivan slipped his little diary out of his inside pocket. On leafing through it he found the two pages at the back he was looking for. One of them was titled, "Last year, 1967," and the other, "Next year, 1969."

Scanning the 1969 page, Ivan realised that it was going to be like all the other years he had ever known. There were just going to be twelve months in it. Concluding that summer would probably be a better time to get married than winter, he said, "What about the mad month? July?"

"Yes, that would likely be a good month," Sylvia replied. "But what day of the month?"

When he had been looking at his diary he noticed that the eleventh of July in the next year would be a Saturday. So he was provided with a ready answer to that enquiry.

"What about the eleventh? Bonfire night. We will really go mad and celebrate!"

"What time will we have it at?"Sylvia persisted.

The questions were coming think and fast now. Sylvia's appetite had been whetted by this wedding talk.

"High Noon," replied Ivan.

His bride-to-be accepted his decision on time without comment. She knew that he was being just a little facetious in his response, but she ignored it. Noon would be as good a time as any.

"What church? Where will we have it, do you think?" she continued.

Ivan was stymied this time. He hadn't planned on a wedding with any religious connotations. A registry office somewhere would have suited him fine.

"I wasn't really thinking about a church," he began to explain, hesitantly. "Anyway, I don't know any ministers." He paused a moment, and then continued, having bethought himself.

"Hold on a minute, I'm telling a lie there. I do know one minister. Only one. He is called the Reverend Billy Vance. He's the minister in the prison."

"Well, I'm certainly not getting married in prison! Not to you or anybody else!" Sylvia's response was immediate, and emphatic.

"No! I don't mean you to get married in prison, stupid!" Ivan was growing impatient. "But Rev. Vance has a church at the corner of Tennant Street. May be he would marry us there if you are all that dead keen on a church. He lives on the North Circular Road. We could go up and see him sometime."

As they were parting, much later that evening, Sylvia announced impishly, "So we will be married on the eleventh of July next year, at high noon, in Tennant Street Presbyterian church if the Reverend Vance will perform the ceremony!"

She had it all cut and dried!

Then her eyes danced and twinkled as she asked, excitedly, "Do you know what that means, Ivan?"

"It means that this time next year I will be your wife!" With that she threw herself into his arms.

Ivan gave her a big kiss, to seal the deal and replied, returning her playful impudence, "Yes, and I will become a 'lifer'!"

From that moment on, Sylvia began to save in earnest. She worked as a stitcher in a factory on the Limestone Road, and was making serious plans for their wedding and future life.

Ivan was different. He loved Sylvia and he really did want to marry her. But he still preferred the butts and the booze to the bows and bouquets.

That was to change, but only gradually.

Sylvia's obvious enthusiasm for things matrimonial carried him along. And he played along. He had to. He had proposed to the girl to start with!

One detail that they had to arrange together was the 'church part' of the wedding, as they called it.

Thus it was that one October evening in October 1968, the young couple knocked on the door of Rev. Billy Vance's home in North Circular Road.

A grey-haired gentleman opened the door.

"Can I help you?" he enquired, with a gracious smile.

"I really hope so," Ivan replied.

Realising that the young man and woman before him were in need of assistance of some sort, and not wanting to interview them on the doorstep, he invited them in.

"Well, come on in and tell me about it," he said, warmly.

When they had made themselves comfortable in the living room, Ivan came straight to the point. There was no need to keep the man waiting.

"My fiancee and I would like you to marry us in your church next year, if that would be possible," he said.

Billy Vance was puzzled. He looked across at the young pair on the settee. There were a number of questions running through his mind.

He needed some answers, some background information.

"Do you attend our church?" he began. When there was no answer to that one he continued with, "Have you been to any of my services? How do you know me?"

Ivan had anticipated some kind of minor cross-examination. When you came to think of it, weren't they two absolute strangers in Vance's manse?

"I never missed one of your Sunday morning services in six months," he stated, truthfully.

The friendly minister looked closely at Ivan without speaking and then a glimmer of recognition seemed to clear his clouded vision.

"I remember you from somewhere," he said, at last. "Where was it again? You will have to refresh my memory. I see so many people you know ..."

"Down the road," explained Ivan, "The Crumlin Road I mean. The prison."

"Oh yes indeed!" Rev. Vance recognised him now, and appeared genuinely pleased to renew his acquaintance. He told his captive congregation every Sunday morning that he would like to see them again 'when they got out'.

Here was one of them now. 'Out', and sitting on his settee.

When Ivan and Sylvia renewed their request to him he was more than happy to comply.

So Ivan and Sylvia were married, exactly as they had planned it, on that balmy August evening, almost a year before ...

At high noon,

On Saturday 11th July, 1969.

In Tennant Street Presbyterian Church,

By Rev. William Vance ...

After the wedding the newly weds moved in with granny. It was cramped in the small flat, but they were happy, all three of them.

Sylvia had Ivan, and she didn't mind sharing him with granny.

Ivan had Sylvia whom he loved. Yet he hadn't deserted the woman who had devoted the latter part of her life to rearing him, through thick and thin.

Granny was a winner in every way. She still had the grandson she cared about under her roof, and she had gained a grand-daughter-in-law to care for her in declining health.

After a few months Ivan and Sylvia rented a flat in the Rathcoole Housing Estate, on the northern outskirts of Belfast. They went there at weekends quite often, leaving granny's daughter, Ivan's aunt, to tend to her ageing mother.

For over a year this arrangement worked well. There was an easy coming-to-terms for everyone. Sylvia was adjusting to married life and granny was adjusting to the little bit of extra 'stir', as she called it. As for Ivan, he was trying, albeit unsuccessfully, to shake the pull of the bookies from his person and his purse.

Then one morning in March, 1971 something dramatic happened.

Granny just took to her bed. Despite earnest coaxings from Ivan and Sylvia she simply refused to rise.

This was most ungranny like.

She had been up early every morning. Helping with the breakfast, helping the young couple to get out.

Even more peculiar than her refusal to get up, was her next request.

She said to her worried grandson, as he stood in a kind of stupor, gazing at her fragile frame in the bed, "Get a doctor, Ivan."

This was something quite uncanny. Granny didn't believe in doctors, as a rule. She had her own personal, tried-and-tested remedies for almost any ailment.

There was no malady with her that couldn't be cured by either a day or two in bed with a hot water bottle, a couple of aspirins and a hot drink, a whiff of Vick, or a dose of syrup of figs. These trusty treatments, used either singly or in any sensible combination, were to her the cure for all ills.

You took the stuff, and the sickness "took its course." And eventually you felt better.

No, granny wasn't big on doctors. She hadn't seen one for years.

Now here she was, asking for one!

Ivan knew that there must be something seriously wrong. Without question he contacted a doctor straight away.

The doctor came down and examined granny carefully. Then he made a few telephone calls, and within an hour an ambulance was at the door.

Granny was going into Whiteabbey Hospital.

Ivan was in a state of shock. He just couldn't believe it.

He travelled with her in the back of the ambulance.

Trying to reassure the little old lady, he took her hand in his and squeezed it tightly.

"Granny, when you get into this hospital they will look after you well, and you will get a good rest. Then you will be a different woman in a couple of weeks."

Granny looked up at him. There was a far-away, yet knowing look about her gaunt complexion.

"When I get down into this hospital son," she replied, "I won't be coming out." She was so calm and measured about it. No big fuss.

This was IT. She knew.

Ivan's mind couldn't cope with it. It wasn't happening as far as he was concerned.

This was the woman who had sheltered him under her shawl as a baby. She had been his champion in the battles of life, his harbour in its storms.

"Nonsense, granny," he continued. He was trying to convince himself, more than her. "They will give you a lot of pills and things and you won't know yourself in a fortnight."

Struggling to make herself comfortable, granny gave a shallow sigh.

"Be a good husband to Sylvia, son. I'm finished!" she said slowly.

When his granny was admitted to Whiteabbey Hospital, Ivan didn't leave her bedside. He sat with her all through that day, and the following night.

During the next day the family gathered. Sylvia was there, his father was there, his aunt was there ... But Ivan was too occupied with the weak little person in the bed to be totally aware of anything else.

Once when her breathing seemed to become more laboured he said to the nurse in attendance, out of sheer frustration and helplessness, "Is my granny in pain?"

By way of an illustration of her answer the nurse leaned over and squeezed the lobe of granny's left ear tightly between her finger and thumb.

There was no reaction.

"See, your grandmother is not in any pain," she whispered comfortingly.

That, at least, was good to know.

Later that evening, with the family gathered around in a strange sense of silent expectation of something unwelcome, granny's breathing became weaker, but more rhythmical.

Then it became even more faint.

There was one final heave.

And the breathing stopped.

Everyone sat stunned, listening to the silence.

Granny was gone.

It was the 10th March, 1971 and Ivan Thompson's world had collapsed.

His granny had been more than his granny to him.

She had been his father, and mother and brother and sister and closest friend. She had been his everything in his early years.

Someone who had known the worst about him - and loved him just the same.

Two days later he stood at the open grave and the coffin was lowered into it. Ivan's tears followed it down. He stood there and wept unashamedly.

The gospel had been preached at that funeral service. Ivan's father had seen to that. But it didn't register with Ivan. He wasn't going to let any of that 'Bible-thumping' get to him, whatever the circumstances.

There was a message, however, that he couldn't escape.

It wasn't the text of the speaker, but it was the implication of the situation.

It was this 'dying' thing.

He had never even entertained the thought of his granny's death. In some naive way he must have expected her just to be there forever. But she wasn't.

Where did that leave him?

The grave seemed to say, "And what about you?"

"You are not here forever, Ivan."

"Someday it is going to be you."

Walking out of the cemetery that day, he resolved to force thoughts of death right out of his mind.

There was only himself and Sylvia for it now.

He would forget about death, and concentrate on life.

He would make the most of ever pound and every minute, to satisfy his every pleasure.

Rathcoole, and riotous living, here we come!

8

The Big Find

Now that granny had passed away, the relationship between Ivan and Sylvia became more strained. There was no mediator now.

There was nobody to whisper to Ivan, now and again, "Give Sylvia a wee bit more consideration, son. She is doing her best for the both of you, you know."

There was nobody to sit with Syliva through the long evenings when her husband was at the greyhound stadium or in the pub, and soothe the situation with statements like, "He has had a hard time," or "He always liked an odd drink," or "He hopes to make is fortune some day on them dogs ..."

The go-between had gone for good.

Rows developed. They increased in frequency and ferocity.

Sylvia's mother was putting a strain on the marriage, totally unwittingly. She was asking, quite reasonably, as she presumed, whey she wasn't ever invited down to see their new flat.

Her question had a simple answer, which only Ivan and Sylvia knew, but which they couldn't explain to mother or mother-in-law.

They would have been much too embarrassed to invite Sylvia's mother or indeed any of their friends or relatives, to see where they lived.

Flat 9D, Abbotscoole House, had hardly anything in it!

They had a bed to sleep in, a sofa to sit on, a TV to look at and a few bits and pieces in the kitchen, and that was all. There was nothing else!

There was no other furniture, they had no floor coverings, and the few curtains there were had been left by a previous tenant, possibly two or three back.

Ivan drank and gambled all his earnings.

Sylvia tried to guard her money, carefully, as she was attempting to feed the pair of them. She was also the one who had to keep constantly bluffing her mother, making all kinds of crazy excuses.

This was a big pressure.

The marriage was been subjected to severe stress. Sylvia was doing her best, as a clean-living industrious wife - but she felt isolated. She knew she was getting nowhere.

It was a blessing that there was somebody who cared.

That somebody was Linda Wright, who worked with her. Sylvia had been a stitcher in Ewing's shirt factory on the Limestone Road in Belfast for many years. The girls who worked with her knew her well, and could sense that she was "about to crack up" as they put it.

However, Linda Wright and some of the other women said that they knew the answer to Sylvia's problems, and to anybody else's problems, for that matter.

That answer, they claimed, was Jesus Christ and faith in Him.

Linda and her friends used to tell Sylvia about how they had found peace and satisfaction through trusting in Jesus. They also used to assure her that they were "praying for" her.

This puzzled Sylvia. Why should they be praying for her? Praying for Ivan, yes, probably. That would be O.K. He had a problem or two, and could be a problem in himself. She could sort of understand them praying for him. Maybe. But for her, who was working as hard as she could, and had no serious vices ... Funny?

When she mentioned it to Ivan one evening he was bitterly sarcastic. "Oh isn't that really nice of them," he sneered, "I'm sure that's bound to help you!"

Ivan had no contact with Christian matters now at all. His father's witness had been buried with granny. There was no communication between them whatsoever, and that was the way Ivan wanted it.

There were constant arguments between him and the longsuffering Sylvia. She was working as much overtime as she could to make as much money as she could. He was squandering every penny he could lay his hands on, his or hers, it didn't matter, in every possible way that he could.

Tension continued to mount.

Pressure was building up to dangerous levels. An escape valve would have to be opened to let off the surplus steam or there was going to be a violent explosion ...

It was an autumn Saturday. Early October 1971. There was an air of suspense and unrest about the city of Belfast. "The troubles" were reaching new depths of horror.

Ivan and Sylvia were walking up the Antrim Road. Sylvia had spent more than half-an-hour standing shivering outside a 'bookies' shop while her husband had gambled away the last of his money, yet again.

They walked into the Waterworks. This had been a favourite haunt of theirs in their younger days. The swans that had sailed so serenely across the water in summer were beginning to look tatty now. Bits of stick, the first of the autumn leaves, and the occasional Coke can floated and bobbed about on the surface.

The sullen couple picking their way over the puddle-strewn paths were totally unaware of their surroundings.

They had their own 'troubles'. Relationships between them were at an all-time low.

Sylvia was at it again. Nagging away. "The old hobby-horse" as Ivan often described it.

"It's an absolute disgrace, Ivan," she was saying, "Look how long I have been working, and what have I to show for it? We haven't got a decent stick of furniture in our flat, and I can't even have my OWN MOTHER down to visit!"

She ended up screaming at him.

They walked on in awkward silence for five minutes. When Sylvia had regained her composure she started to say things like, "It's pointless this marriage. We are not getting any pleasure from it, either of us. We may as well pack it in ..."

Ivan allowed her to rant on and on. They walked out of the Waterworks into Queen Mary's Gardens.

Sylvia was now very upset again. She was sobbing and sniffling, dabbing at her eyes and nose with a semi-saturated ball of a handkerchief.

Feeling that he could take no more of this, Ivan had just his mouth open to say, "Well, whatever you like then. I f you want to call it a day ..." Sylvia forestalled him.

"I'm going in here to the 'Ladies', she announced suddenly. With that she left her dejected husband and walked quickly towards the public toilets.

Ivan waited outside for her. She wouldn't be long.

He sat on the edge of the raised concrete platform on which the public conveniences had been built. And he waited.

When he became chilled sitting there he got up stiffly and walked about a bit, stamping his feet and blowing his hands to restore the circulation and warm himself up.

Still Sylvia didn't come out. Still he waited.

Could she have done something stupid?

Was she lying in there with her wrists slashed and blood all over the place?

Had she taken an overdose?

Had she decided to end it all? She had been very distressed when she went in.

Impatience got the better of him. Although he had been cruelly unkind to Sylvia he still loved her very much. He didn't want anything to happen to her.

Ivan decided that some action was called for. He had waited far too long. Glancing around in all directions to make sure nobody was looking he slipped inside the door of the 'Ladies'. A concrete wall faced him. He was just about to sneak a peep around it when he heard movement.

Good, Sylvia was coming.

Turning quickly, he retreated, back to sitting down, trying to appear unconcerned.

But it wasn't Sylvia! A strange woman came out of the ladies toilet, did a detour to come round past him, and gave him the longest fiercest stare he had seen for some time!

Still he waited. Still no Sylvia.

He looked at what remained of the summer floral display. A few brave blooms were trying to hold their heads up, despite the autumn chill. He admired them, for he was almost numb with cold.

Eventually, after what seemed to him like endless ages, Sylvia emerged. After the anxiety of that lonely wait, Ivan was determined that he was going to be nice to her, for a while at least.

The wife who had entered the public conveniences weeping came out much later still weeping. Now there was something different though.

She had a big broad smile on her face as well. Sylvia was smiling through her tears.

How could she even dare to look happy?

Ivan's first thought was, "She has found a purse in there. Probably with a lot of money in it." Their problems would all be solved.

Since Sylvia hadn't spoken yet, Ivan opened the conversation, putting his theory to the test.

"Hey, Sylvia, you are starting to look happy again. Did you find a purse in there, or what?"

Looking across to meet his gaze, his reanimated wife replied with deep conviction, "No Ivan, but I have found the Saviour."

That declaration stopped him dead in his tracks!

Ivan grabbed her by the arm and just stared and stared at her. He was dumbfounded.

After a few mesmerised minutes, Ivan lifted his right arm weakly and pointed back in he direction of Queen Mary's Gardens.

"In there?" he asked, not believing what he had just heard, not knowing what to say next.

"Yes, in there," Sylvia replied, starting to walk on, up the Antrim Road. A few hurried steps allowed Ivan to catch up with her again.

"The girls in work have been talking to me about the Lord," Sylvia began to explain.

"Oh, yes, likely the ones that were 'praying for' you." Ivan's sarcasm had only mildly abated.

"Yes indeed," Sylvia continued, taking no notice. "They were the ones who told me about Jesus. They told me that He died for me and that I need to come to Him. He could give me rest, they said. In those toilets back there I just came to that place where I gave my whole life to Him. I know he will make me His child, and give me peace."

Ivan didn't like this at all. His wife was beginning to sound like his father, whom he had been trying to avoid. So he kept up the arguments.

Right up the Antrim Road they walked and talked. Then they went down O'Neill Road towards Rathcoole.

The lights of Holywood and Bangor were twinkling, across the other side of Belfast Lough, as evening approached. They saw nothing.

The exchanges between them were different, however, and Ivan couldn't understand it. There was another worrying aspect about their relationship now.

To every contentious issue that Ivan advanced, trying to draw Sylvia into some hasty, fiery response, she just replied, "Oh, is that right?" or "That's probably true ..."

His Sylvia had changed dramatically.

There was no fight left in her now. No struggle. She seemed like a different person.

A new creature!

As they were going up in the lift to their flat, Ivan looked intently at Sylvia again. Her face was glowing, having come in from the cold. The sparkle had returned to her sad-for-along-time eyes.

He knew how to cope with an argument.

He knew how to cope with a row.

He could even handle himself in a full-blown fight.

But how did you cope with this?

The next day was Sunday and they were spending it together in the flat. Ivan decided that he would change his approach to his wife. He would adopt a "softly-softly" approach and try to talk her through this "religious" phase.

They were sitting on the settee, watching the TV when Ivan remarked casually, "Do you know what happened to you yesterday, Sylvia? Your nerves have taken a turn for the worse. You have turned to religion as a way out. Some people turn to drugs. Some go to the Citizen's Advice Bureau. You have just gone religious. But don't let it take over you, Sylvia. Don't get fanatical about it, I mean. It's just your nerves."

He made a final gesture with his hands, preparing to resign the whole matter of Sylvia and her 'religion' to oblivion.

Sylvia stood up and faced her husband. Positioning herself between Ivan and the TV, she drew herself up to every inch of her five foot nothing.

Then with that placid smile which she had rediscovered the day before, she said curiously,"So it's my nerves is it? That is really choice! Look at you, Ivan. You are smoking sixty cigarettes a day. You have the nails chewed completely off yourself ..."

She took a few steps towards the kitchen door, then stopped. Looking down at him with an inquisitive grin, she fired her final shot.

"Think hard now," she began, "Then tell me. Whose nerves do you think are away?!"

9

"You Will Be In Hell"

October progressed.

The change that had taken place in Sylvia's life began to show in her surroundings. She bought simple items to enhance their dismal flat.

Ivan noticed that.

The biggest change, however, was in her attitude and behaviour.

He noticed that too.

Each evening, Sylvia sat reading a little Bible which the women in work had given to her. They had been delighted to hear her tell of how she had come to the Saviour and encouraged her, promising to help her in every possible way.

When she had finished reading the Bible, she closed it gently, and slipped down on to her knees at the sofa. There she prayed quietly.

Linda Wright became a spiritual guide to Sylvia. Her advice was sound, only one part of it Sylvia thought could never be achieved. Linda had said that she should read the Bible and pray. Both of these she was doing and deriving great comfort from them.

The third piece of advice that Sylvia had been given was that she should get Ivan to take her to church sometime.

That would just be out of the question, she thought!

Ivan had no intention of taking her to church. Her constant consistent witnessing aggravated him.

On his way home from work he used to think, "If Sylvia is reading that Bible or praying instead of making my dinner, I will soon tell her what I think of her Christianity!"

Sylvia made sure he didn't have any need to say such things. She would greet him with, "Oh hello, love. It's great to see you home again. Your dinner is in the oven. I will get if for you now."

With that she would go into the kitchen, and come out again a few minutes later, with a tasty dinner for both of them.

Instead of Ivan being pleased about this, it annoyed him. There was no fight in Sylvia now, not even the occasional swear word.

She was so good, so kind, so 'holy' ...

One evening Ivan was in the bathroom, preparing to go out.

Suddenly the door opened and he came storming out clutching a handful of tracts, which he waved above his head.

"It's beginning to look like a monastery in here," he yelled. "There are even religious books on the cistern now! Can a man not go into his own toilet in peace?!"

After a final flourish he opened his hand to allow the booklets to fall and flutter to the floor.

Smiling, Sylvia began to pick them up.

"I just thought you would like something to read in ...", she was beginning to explain.

Her explanations were unheard.

There was a thunderous bang of a door.

Everything in the flat rattled.

Ivan was back in a tract-free-bathroom.

He used to mock her mercilessly when she prayed.

Sylvia was kneeling silently at their well-worn settee, praying silently, one Sunday afternoon. Her Bible, which she had been reading earlier, lay beside her.

Ivan decided that he would shame her out of this praying fad. Going across to the big swing-over window in the flat, he opened it and leaned out. When he was as far out as he could go, without falling out on his head, he shouted back over his shoulder, "Sylvia, who are you talking to anyway? There's nobody out here! There's nothing out here but clouds and seagulls!"

To allow Sylvia to reap the benefit of this caustic comment, he paused for a few moments.

There was no sound. No movement. No reply.

Then he glanced back into the living room.

Sylvia was still on her knees.

He would yell on undeterred. Somebody out there would hear him, and sympathise with him, for the religious fanatic of a wife that he was stuck with. That would surely stop her.

"I can't see any God out here!" he bawled, "Wouldn't you think that if there was a God about anywhere you could see him from nine storeys up?! ..."

Ivan joked and jeered, scoffed and sneered, for the next five minutes.

Sylvia prayed silently on.

Eventually he was forced to give up. It was cold out there in his shirt-sleeves, he was beginning to feel sick from hanging down out of the window, and the lower metal bar of the frame had made a half-inch furrow across both thighs.

Sylvia, and God, had won again.

How desperately frustrating!

Ivan was so exasperated by his wife because he was convicted by her. He knew that the way she was behaving now was different. It was an improvement. It was right!

He knew that what she was saying now was different as well, but it was absolutely true.

Ivan didn't admit to these realisations to anybody. They just pierced him through the heart.

It was the stark truth of something that she said one evening, that really got to him!

It was a Saturday. Ivan often went out with his mates on a Saturday evening - down to the Merville Inn for a drink.

On that particular evening three of them came knocking at the door of the flat. They were looking for Ivan.

Their drinking partner-to-be said to them, "Just wait in the hallway there, lads. I will be with you in a minute."

History was about to repeat itself.

A few years before, some of his friends had crowded into the entrance hall of the little flat in Hanna Street, to wait for him. Ivan had come out of that flat, challenged to live the Christian life as it should be lived - and show up "all the hypocrites" for what they were.

On that Crazy Beat occasion it had been his father who had confronted him with the claims of Christ.

He hadn't liked it.

This evening it was to be his wife who would speak a timely word to him.

He wasn't going to like this either.

Having made hurried visits to the bedroom and the bathroom, to add the finishing touches to his titivation, Ivan came out through the living room. After nodding to his three friends to proceed out on to the landing, he followed them, shooing them forward with his two hands spread out, like a farmer willing sheep to go through a gap.

When they were all out, Ivan turned to his patient wife, who was standing in the middle of the living room floor. His hand clutched the handle of the outside door.

"We are away now, Sylvia," he called, "And I don't know what time I will be back at!"

Sylvia was worried for him. She had never known what time he would 'be back at'. Things were worse now, though. The troubles were intensifying. Some husbands, in their circles, just didn't return at all.

Her deep concern was reflected in her next remark.

"Don't be letting anything happen to you, love," she said gently. "You'll be in hell, you know."

Ivan didn't reply. He just slammed the front door shut, and followed his pals into the lift.

As that lift travelled swiftly groundwards he could not banish those parting words from his minds. Every time it clattered and faltered as it passed another floor, Ivan flinched.

Down, down, down they went.

The sinking lift spoke loudly.

"You," it said.

"Will be," it said.

"In hell," it said.

When they reached the pub it was crowded, noisy and very busy.

Normally Ivan would have been 'the life and soul' of the party. He was usually a prime mover in all the chat and action.

Tonight he was just plain miserable.

As he sat glumly at the bar, staring into space, one of his mates came up to him. After sitting in silence beside Ivan for a few tortuous minutes, he ventured to ask, genuinely, "Hey, Ivan, what's wrong with you? You are not your jolly old self tonight."

"My jolly old self!" Ivan replied angrily. The venom of his retort startled his friend.

"My jolly old self! Did you hear what Sylvia said to me before I left that flat?" he continued.

"No, I didn't." His pal was puzzled by all this.

"What was it? What did she say?" he asked, then added, "Whatever it was it seems to have got you right and mad!"

"She said, 'Don't let anything happen to you, love. You will be in hell!' Ivan was really incensed by now. He couldn't get it out of his mind. His friend had summed it up correctly. He was 'right and mad'.

Afraid that everyone in the crowded lounge would hear Ivan's outburst, his pal tried to calm him down, saying sympathetically, "I don't like the sound of that!"

"Well neither do I," Ivan answered tersely. "And I am going to put a stop to it."

Banging his almost empty glass down on the bar, he fumed on, "I can tell you there will be no more holy advice by the time I am finished. There will be no more of this praying. No more tracts! No more religion rammed down my throat!"

Slipping down off the bar-stool, Ivan buttoned up his overcoat, slowly and deliberately. Then turning to his bewildered mate, he said emphatically, "Cheerio, I'm away! I'm going home to sort a few things out ..."

The swinging door swung back, then forward.

There was an awkward silence.

Ivan had gone. Home. "To sort a few things out."

10

The Lady's Choice

Sylvia was startled to hear a key in the lock. She had been dozing in front of the TV, but came to her senses with a jolt.

Surely that couldn't be Ivan back so soon!

"Is he all right?" she began to wonder. "He certainly seemed in good enough form when he left."

Those questions were soon to be answered.

Her harassed husband hit the living room like a raging bull.

Totally ignoring Sylvia's, "It's good to see you back so soon, love. Is there any thing wrong?" he bulldozed past her as she stood up to greet him. When he had charged down into the bedroom he pulled an old battered case down from the top of the wardrobe.

He was going to teach this goody-goody wife of his a lesson! Once and for all!

Returning to the living-room, after a toilet stop, Ivan brandished the case.

"I'm getting out of here!" he shouted, "I have had enough of this! You are not the woman I married!"

"You are right about that, love," Sylvia replied, meekly. "I know things have changed."

"And you are dead right about that, I may say!" Ivan roared in return. "Things HAVE changed. You don't want to go where I want to go any more! You don't want to do what I want to do any more! Well I can take no more of it! I'm leaving!"

"Oh Ivan, love, where would you go to?" Sylvia was on the verge of tears.

"I will go to some place where there is no more preaching. No more praying. No more Bibles. And no tracts staring at you every time you turn round ...!" was the instant response.

Just as he was making a show of going towards the outside door Sylvia spoke, with trembling voice.

"Ivan, you are asking me to choose the Lord, or to choose you," she said simply.

"Put it whatever way you like!" Ivan countered.

Then he hesitated, thoughtfully.

He hadn't realised it was as stark a choice as that.

An unseen force restrained him.

Setting the case down on the floor, but still holding on to the handle, he looked up at Sylvia. He could see the tears welling up in her eyes.

"What an awful thing for you to say!" he continued, in a more controlled manner than he had yet displayed since his rowdy return.

"But that IS what you are asking me, Ivan. I must either give Him up, or give you up," Sylvia persisted firmly.

The tears were now flowing down her cheeks and glistening on her chin. She made no effort to wipe them away.

After only a brief pause she looked fixedly at her husband, and announced with quiet determination, "I'm choosing the Lord!"

With that she collapsed on to the settee, and burying her head in her hands, she sobbed on rhythmically.

The power left Ivan's legs. His speech dried up.

His arms began to shake, uncontrollably.

He knew nothing about Moses and his choice.

He knew nothing about Joshua and his choice.

But he now knew about Sylvia and her choice.

And it had fairly knocked all the fight out of him!

Feeling defeated and humiliated, but not daring to wave the white flag of surrender, he wanted to have the last word.

"Well, I'll not leave tonight then Sylvia. But I'm warning you!" His final threat had about as much lethal power as a big bang from a cap gun. He knew that.

Being totally in a quandary as to know what to do or say next, he picked up the suitcase and crept like a chastened child back to the bedroom.

With funny hollow arms he swung the suit case back on to the top of the wardrobe.

It was empty. Like his heart.

He hadn't put a single thing in that case. He had never really intended to go away. His plan had been to scare sense into Sylvia.

It hadn't worked.

It had backfired, badly.

Ivan threw himself down on the bed. Cupping his hands behind his head, he stared up at the ceiling. It hadn't been painted for years. That didn't concern him now. There were more pressing problems on his mind.

His whole being was in turmoil. His heart had been torn apart by Sylvia's bold statement of loyalty to her Lord.

"What am I going to do?" he wondered to himself.

"We haven't resolved anything. My bluff has been called. I am out of ammunition. What AM I going to do?"

11

It's Later Than You Think

A short time had elapsed from that fateful Saturday night, when Sylvia decided to press home her advantage. She knew that God and she were making an impression.

Ivan hadn't left home.

He continued to scorn and threaten.

He continued to scoff and taunt.

But he didn't leave. Sylvia knew now that he wouldn't.

One evening as they sat by the fire after dinner, Sylvia suggested the unthinkable.

"You haven't taken me to church yet Ivan. You are a disgrace. All the girls in work go to church with their boyfriends and husbands. But not me. Oh no! I just have to say, 'I don't think Ivan would be interested.' Mind you I would really love to go." she said.

She knew her husband well. He wasn't interested. Her accurate assessment of the situation gave Ivan the opportunity to reply.

"You are correct," he began. "I am not interested. I wouldn't go to church. Were you ever in one of them places, Sylvia? Did you know that the women in there wear dead dogs round their necks?"

Sylvia laughed at him.

"Those are fox-furs," she replied. "Not dead dogs. Now what's your excuse, Ivan?"

"This is no excuse, Sylvia, I am telling you the truth," he continued, warming to the topic. Any chance at all to poke fun at Christians or churches was always welcome.

"The people who go to church all think that they are somebody. They drive big cars and wear swanky clothes. Pack of snobs the whole lot of them!"

"Nonsense, Ivan. Lies again." Sylvia smiled patiently as she answered. Then she dropped the subject, but only temporarily.

A few nights later she tried a different approach.

Ivan was leafing through a newspaper in the living room. He only bought papers for the horse-racing pages. It was important to study the form.

"Ivan, I would like you to do something for me," Sylvia called through to him from the kitchen. She reckoned that he was in a reasonably good mood that evening.

Her husband wasn't going to be fooled by any please-darling-just-for-me type charm. He knew the signs. He saw it coming.

"Yes," he shouted back, anticipating her request. "I know. Take me to church."

Sylvia appeared through into the living room. She was grinning. "That's right, love. How did you guess? Take me to church." she said, repeating his words.

After all her apparently futile badgering she was totally unprepared for Ivan's response.

Folding the paper, he looked up at her and asked, simply, "Well, where do you want to go?"

Leaning against the wall for support, Sylvia tried to appear serene. She had just received the surprise of her life.

"There's a church round the corner," she was pleased to inform him. "It is called Abbots Cross Congregational. They tell me that there is a good preacher round there."

Despite his relentless ridicule, Ivan didn't know much about churches. He only pretended that he did.

"Are there many goes?" he asked

"O yes, I believe its packed," his wondering wife responded readily. She couldn't credit that Ivan was talking about church without contempt.

Her husband's imagination ran riot on the 'packed' idea. He could just picture them, jammed in like sardines. He might even find himself staring into a dead dog's glazed eyes.

However, Sylvia had made her choice and he played along with it.

"What time was it at?" Ivan enquired.

"It starts at half-past six," Sylvia told him.

"Well, all right then. I will go with you on Sunday evening," he conceded. "But on one condition."

"What's that?" Sylvia could hardly believe that this was her Ivan talking.

"That is that we go early and get either a front seat or a back seat. I want everybody to see the back of my head, or else I want to see the back of everybody else's head! I'm not going into any packed church!"

The 'one condition' sounded like two to Sylvia, but the terms sounded reasonable enough. She was prepared to go as early as he liked. If he suggested going at four o'clock in the afternoon she would be happy to comply.

"Whatever you want," she replied, gratefully.

Next Sunday would be the 31st October.

Between the evening of his amazing promise and the Sunday when it was due to be kept, Ivan had bought the Radio Times. He found out, to his dismay, that there was going to be a special film on the TV for Halloween.

'Moby Dick, The Great White Whale' was due to be screened on Sunday 31st October at 7:00 pm.

Ivan would really like to see the film. But what could he do? He had made a promise to Sylvia, and he would have to keep it.

Having turned it over in his mind for a few hours, he had a brain-wave. He remembered Granny, and a trick of hers.

They had an alarm clock in Hanna Street, but Ivan used to lie in beyond the alarm. He loved those last minutes in bed. So granny, in an effort to get her bed-loving grandson to work on time, used to put the clock forward by fifteen or twenty minutes. When the alarm went off Ivan used to enjoy those last few precious minutes in bed, and still be in time to have breakfast and get to work easily.

What if he were to practice a bit of clock-tampering on their single timepiece? Only instead of putting the clock forward, he would put it back, say half-an-hour. Then if they left the flat at six o'clock with their clock it would really be half-past six. It could work.

Hadn't Sylvia agreed that he wouldn't have to go into a packed church?

Meanwhile, much to his wife's amazement, Ivan went through all he motions. He even had his hair cut and bought a new tie to wear!

On the Sunday afternoon when Sylvia was elsewhere in the flat he did a granny-in-reverse job on the clock. It was a state of the art silver model with two bells on top that went bang! bang! bang! when it alarmed.

He put it back half-an-hour. Suddenly, a quarter-past three became a quarter -to three. Then he spent the remainder of the afternoon in fear and trepidation in case Sylvia would notice.

She didn't.

While they were having something eat, around five o'clock, Sylvia asked, still afraid that he might change his mind, "What time will we leave at for church, love?"

"Oh, it won't take us any more than five minute s to walk around there," was Ivan's long considered reply. "We will leave about six o'clock. That should leave us plenty of time to be there good and early."

That's exactly what they did. Having dressed themselves up like they hadn't been dressed for a long time before, they left at six o'clock by the clock on the fireplace, to walk round to Abbots Cross Congregational Church.

What a sight met their gaze when they came close to the church, however!

The car park was crammed with cars. A few people were still anxiously driving up and down the road outside, searching for somewhere to park.

"So far, so good," thought Ivan.

As he tried to slow the pace of their progress, Sylvia marched strongly forward. When they had walked up through the crowded car park they approached the door of the church.

Looking in through the open front doors, Ivan and Sylvia could see people standing in the porch. Busy men, in suits, were carrying chairs from another room somewhere, in an attempt to pack the last few people in.

At last Sylvia began to slow down. She looked mystified.

"What's happening here?" she finally asked, with her breath coming in short gasps. "We left in plenty of time."

"I don't know what has happened here," Ivan replied, "But what I do want to know is, what kind of a place this is, that the people all come so early?"

"There must be some mistake," his wife concluded, advancing doorwards again, dragging Ivan after her. "It must be later than we think."

Ivan tried to halt her onward course, by stopping dead in he car park.

"Now Sylvia," he said, appealing to her Christianity. "You wouldn't expect me to go in there. Would you now? Remember our deal. I wasn't to be asked to go into any packed church."

He knew Sylvia to have a sense of honour and decency. She would keep her end of the bargain, he was sure. Moby Dick, here we come!

Although he was aware of his wife's sense of fair play, he also knew her to be a very determined little lady.

It was her determination that took the joystick that evening in the car park.

She tightened her grip on Ivan's arm. He refused to budge.

If he wasn't going in, she wasn't going home.

Human tug of war ensued.

Ivan was heading out of the car park.

Sylvia was heading into the church. Each was trying to pull the other in the opposite direction.

"Let go of my arm!" Ivan shouted. He was becoming really angry.

"That's a real Christian thing you are doing I might say, pulling me about like that!"

Jimmy Carson had been standing in the porch, handing out hymn-books. He heard the commotion in the car park, and quick as a flash he was out to investigate. Jimmy was a tough man, broad as a door, with a grip like Big Daddy.

Looking at the struggling couple he asked, "What's the problem here?"

"I can't get him in," Sylvia panted almost in despair. She sounded like a frustrated mother, trying to get her reluctant offspring into the house for bed on a warm and sunny summer evening.

Jimmy took a step closer. Trying to allay Ivan's fears, he said with genuine warmth, "We are really glad to see you!"

"Glad to see me! You needn't be glad to see me! I'm not staying here!" yelled Ivan back at him.

"Why not?" Jimmy's expression had changed from one of welcome to one of wonder.

The respite with the intervening churchman had allowed Sylvia time to regain her composure.

"He wanted a seat at the front," she explained, trying to excuse his irrational behaviour.

Before Jimmy could even reply, Ivan butted in. "You would have no chance of getting any seat at all in there," he said, slightly calmer. "I will come back next week."

Having been released from Sylvia's clutches, he turned to walk away. Jimmy Carson was having none of it.

Grabbing Ivan firmly by both wrists he said, "Never worry. You will be all right!" With that he made resolutely towards the church door.

Ivan was in shock. He was so stunned that he didn't even resist. His captor had him in a vice-like grip.

Up the steps they went, through the porch and up the aisle of the church. Jimmy, leading Ivan, led the way. They carved out a course for themselves, like a ship through an ocean, leaving Sylvia to churn along in their foaming wake. Her well-brushed hair was now blown and tousled. Her face was flushed with excitement. She was wondering just what was going to happen next.

Astonished people were brushed aside by the advancing trio. Those who didn't scuttle away like frightened mice were knocked over like skittles.

Jimmy Carson was bringing his prize to the front of the church. If it was a front seat he wanted, it would be a front seat he would get!

Having reached the front row, Jimmy somehow found two seats right in the middle of it. After directing Ivan and Sylvia to be seated, he handed them a hymn book each.

Just as Ivan was sitting down, wondering what all of this was about, Jimmy hit him a resounding thump on the back and shouted "Glory!" at the top of his voice.

All the air in Ivan's body rushed out in one big whoosh! He sat there dazed, stupefied and breathless.

He couldn't believe that he had allowed this to happen.

Sylvia sat glowing. She was overjoyed, but breathless, too.

She couldn't believe that her husband had allowed this to happen either.

Her many fervent prayers had been answered.

Her fondest wish had been realised.

Linda Wright's seemingly impossible advice had become an incredible reality.

Ivan Thompson was in a church!

Right below the pulpit!

12

Just As You Are

Sylvia was as happy as a lark. Ivan was as cross as a bear.

Sylvia was radiant. Ivan was raging.

Here he was, right up at the front of a church, within an arm's length of the pulpit. And there was something even worse. All his carefully laid plans had gone awry. He was going to miss Moby Dick.

Another backfire.

The most galling aspect of the whole situation for him, however, was the fact that everybody around him seemed to be like Sylvia. They all seemed so keen and so glad to be present. There was a shiny-faced, eager-eyed expectancy about the place.

The singing impressed Ivan. He had never even heard half of the hymns and choruses before but everyone around him seemed to know them all, and their tunes, off by heart.

Just one person annoyed him. There was a wee old pensioner sitting at the end of the row behind them and he shouted "Hallelujah" at the end of every chorus.

"What kind of an odd-ball is that?" thought Ivan. "He must be doting - or may be he is a bit simple."

Deliberate stony stares made no difference to the little man or his exclamations. He just continued with his predictable but provoking outbursts.

Giving up on the Hallelujah chorus, Ivan fixed his attention on an elderly lady to the right of him. She was simply dressed, but she was happy. Really joyful. When she stood up to sing she seemed to want to reach up as close as she could go to heaven, for she stood right up on her tiptoes. She reminded Ivan of a canary stretching up to sing, on the top perch of its cage. "If she falls," he mused, "I will go over and pick her up. She couldn't be too heavy."

The Christian canary looked across and met his gaze. She gave him a full-face smile. With eyes closed, nose wrinkled up and mouth cleaving her countenance from ear to ear, she beamed at him.

She reminded Ivan of granny. Her reassuring warmth comforted him. He felt slightly, but only slightly, more at ease.

When everybody sat down at the end of the hymn, Ivan listened to the announcements. He thought he should listen to something, for he certainly couldn't see anything. The base of the pulpit was singularly un interesting.

The announcements were interesting, though. Ivan had often wondered how these 'religious' people passed their time. Now he knew. They went to prayer meetings, Bible studies, youth rallies. There was even a later service that night in another local church. Imagine anybody wanting to attend TWO church services on the same evening!

After the announcements, a soloist sang two pieces. The words were unfamiliar and the tunes strange. "Good singer though," Ivan decided to himself, "but definitely not a Crazy Beat."

A settled hush fell upon the audience as Rev. Sam Workman rose to speak. He read from the Bible and began to preach.

Ivan switched off. The singing had been peculiar but pleasant, the announcements mildly fascinating, but his preaching was not for him.

It was his father all over again.

It was his wife all over again.

It was all the same old stuff in a different parcel.

He began to look around him, for he couldn't look ahead of him. Did any body else find this whole set up as tedious as he did?

His wandering gaze came to rest on a woman's navy hat. It had a big clump of probably plastic fruit on it. "Good idea, " Ivan thought. "Bring some light refreshment with you. On your hat." Then he began to count the number of women who were wearing hats. He gave up at twenty-seven for he had a crick in his neck with turning round. Anyway he was going to have to stand up to look farther down the church, and he thought 'they' might not like that. Never in his life before had he seen so many hats in one place, not even at a wedding.

There was also a small matter of the dead dogs. He made a mental note to apologise to Sylvia on that one. His intense scrutiny of that church audience, and especially the ladies, hadn't revealed a single canine corpse in the whole place.

Ivan pricked up his ears when he heard the speaker remark, "I must close soon. The clock has beaten us again. But there's just one more thing ..."

That probably meant it would all be over soon.

"Good," Ivan concluded. "I hope all these well-dressed, respectable people enjoyed it. It must have been for them, for it certainly wasn't for me. I'm gambling. I'm smoking. I'm drinking and I'm as crooked as a corkscrew.

I could never be religious like Sylvia or my father or any of these apparently perfect people. There would be too many things in my life to be made right. What would I do about the booze? How could I do without the bookies? And the cigarettes?

No. It's definitely not for me ..."

His inward and silent, but nonetheless determined, rejection of all things spiritual, was interrupted by the speaker's voice.

"That's my message finished," he was saying. As he heard the Bible, almost above his head, close with a gentle creak of the pages, Ivan wondered, "How much of Moby Dick will be left when we get home?"

Again, Ivan was returned to reality by the preacher's voice.

Apparently he hadn't quite finished. There was more. He added a final sentence.

"If you ever want to come to the Lord Jesus, you will have to come just the way you are," he stated emphatically.

Suddenly defiant indifference changed to definite interest. Leaning over to Sylvia, Ivan asked in a stage whisper, "What was that he said?"

Mildly embarrassed but genuinely surprised, Sylvia replied, "He said that you have to come to Jesus just the way you are."

"What does that mean?" Ivan persisted. He wanted to know more and he didn't care who heard him.

His position at the front of the church must have allowed the speaker to hear his eager enquiry. Rev. Workman stretched forward over the edge of the pulpit and repeated his statement, earnestly.

"That's right. If you ever want to become a Christian you will have to come to the Lord Jesus. And come just the way you are."

Ivan's mind was in a whirl. "Just the way I am. Does that mean me, with the drink and the cigarettes? Could Jesus want somebody like me?"

Then dawn began to break in his soul. He realised that it wasn't what he could do would save him. It was what Christ had done. He wasn't expected to give up anything, but Jesus had given up His life to make salvation possible.

All he had to do was come to the Saviour. Just the way he was.

Throughout the closing prayer and benediction Ivan sat with his head bowed. He was a broken, contrite, repentant man.

Humbly and quietly he committed his life to the Lord. Coming 'just as he was,' he thanked Jesus for dying on a cross for him, and asked the Saviour to come into his heart and life.

When Ivan reopened his eyes, tears were streaming down his cheeks onto the floor. People were rising, shuffling, preparing to move out.

Ivan sat still.

When he glanced over at Sylvia, who was still sitting beside him, he noticed that tears were coursing down her flushed cheeks as well!

Ivan whispered into her ear, "I'm saved!"

Turning right round to look full into his face, she replied, with an absolutely radiant smile, "I know!"

"Who told you?" was the new convert's instinctive response.

"Nobody told me. I just KNOW!" Sylvia said happily.

It was obvious to her that the fervent prayers of many Christians for many days and many nights had been answered.

To her Ivan-trained eye, able to predict his every mood and whim, "I'm saved!" was written all over his beaming face in luminous letters.

Ivan jumped up. He felt about five stones lighter. The burdens that had weighed him down for so long had vanished.

Grabbing Sylvia by the hand, he propelled her towards the door. He was motivated into motion by an unseen spiritual energy that he had never experienced before.

It was his turn to do a Jimmy Carson on the patient people moving slowly down the aisles towards the door. Their muted comments of "Great meeting", "very solemn", were interrupted by a big man with a tear-stained face guiding a small woman with a tear-stained face through them. They stood back in awe and let the couple pass.

When they reached the freedom of the car park, that October evening, Ivan lifted his wife off the ground, and swung her round and round, much to the astonishment of the bemused congregation who were beginning to fan out on the church steps.

"The One I scorned! The One I mocked! The One I jeered at!" he was exclaiming. "I have Him in my heart! What a miracle! And all because I came to Him. Just the way I was!"

There was joy in Ivan's heart.

There was joy in Sylvia's heart.

There was joy in the presence of the angels of heaven.

The more conservative Christians, buttoning up their coats and unlocking their cars, nodded knowingly to one another.

There was joy in their hearts as well.

13

God's Taximan

As they moved out of the church car park on to the footpath, Ivan had a spring in his step.

There was a song in his mouth.

He had the Saviour in his heart.

He had been released from he guilt of his sin.

Ivan was so filled with the joy of his salvation that he wanted to hear more, much more, about the Christian life upon which he had just embarked.

What had once been punishment had now become nourishment.

He had listened to those announcements in the service out of curiosity. Now they became a lifeline to him.

Remembering that a further meeting had been announced for later that evening he suddenly found that he had a burning desire to go to it. NOW he could understand people who wanted to attend two church services on the same evening.

He had become one of them.

Setting off along the pavement towards home, Ivan was striding out purposefully a few steps ahead of Sylvia. His wife's heart was full of joy and peace but her feet were tortured with aches and pains. Those brand new and very stiff bought-for-the-occasion shoes must have been a bout a half-size too small. Her toes were crushed into a shapeless mass and her heels were chafed. Attempting to overcome this relatively minor physical affliction she hobbled on happily behind her happy husband.

Half-turning to address her, Ivan said, "You know, Sylvia, there is more of this. The man in that place said that there would be another meeting in Whiteabbey Presbyterian Church at a quarter-past eight. I would really love to go to it."

"O.K. love, that's all right. We will go," Sylvia replied.

If her Ivan wanted "more of this" she would be all for it. It would be better than the booze or the bookies any day, she reckoned.

The practicalities of the situation clouded her dream.

Whiteabbey Presbyterian Church was two miles away, they were on foot, and she was in agony with every step.

She felt compelled to bring the situation down to earth and be a bit more realistic about it.

"That is if we can make it in time," she added.

Ivan was so ecstatic and yet so simple in his newly-found faith that he exclaimed, "I have just given my heart to the Lord. Wouldn't you think that He could get us a taxi?"

Just as he was finishing this apparently ridiculous and unreasonably demanding statement, a car drew up alongside the kerb. The driver leaned across the empty passenger seat and wound down the window.

Ivan and Sylvia stopped.

"I'm a stranger in these parts," the driver began, "Do you know how I would get to Whiteabbey Presbyterian Church? I want to go and hear this man Arthur Blissit."

"No problem," Ivan responded readily. "I know where the church is. I will take you there!"

Then the astonished traveller could only watch and listen open-mouthed while Ivan directed Sylvia, who was by now leaning up against him for support, "Jump into the car there. We will show this man where the church is."

Opening the back door, Ivan waited until his wife climbed into the back seat, and he followed.

As the driver moved off with his newly-acquired passengers, Ivan said to him, "Do you know that you are a taxi, sent by God, to take us to that meeting? I have just got saved ten minutes ago in a church back there, and I was saying to my wife, Sylvia here, 'Wouldn't you think that if God wanted us to go to that other place He would send us a taxi.'"

Summing up the subject, Ivan hit the bewildered motorist a hearty slap on the shoulder and proclaimed, "You may not realise it, my friend, but you are God's taximan!"

The feeling-hi-jacked driver was totally baffled. He was virtually lost for words.

"I'm ... I'm ... a Presbyterian!" he blurted out.

That was to be the extent of his conversation with these two looneys he had lifted. Other than an occasional grunt of "Uh! Huh!" when Ivan said, "Turn right," "Left here," "Straight on up this road," he didn't say any more.

With decisive use of both the accelerator and the brake, he provided the pair of religious freaks with a hair-raising ride to their destination.

Stopping at the first available spot, the would-be-church-goer was pleased to see his passengers alight. Sylvia wasn't too happy to get out though. She had enjoyed the rest, however bumpy it may have been.

After expressing their gratitude to their rather relieved driver, the couple turned their attentions to Whiteabbey Presbyterian Church.

Thanks to the speed of "God's taximan" and Ivan's accurate directions they had arrived in good time for the after-church rally. Although it was still early, crowds were flocking into the church.

Arthur Blissit, who was to be the speaker that evening, had quite a charisma. He had walked through all parts of Belfast transporting a massive wooden cross with a tiny wheel on the back.

Obviously many people wanted to hear him.

Ivan, in his eagerness, rushed ahead of his wife, up the steps. Now Sylvia, who had struggled to get him into the first meeting, lagged behind him, struggling to get herself into the second one.

Her feet were so sore! She felt peculiar. All dressed up with big blisters on her heels.

Before entering the church door, Ivan waited until she had joined him. She assured him that she was extremely happy. And she was, despite everything!

The flamboyant Arthur Blissit was welcoming his prospective congregation.

His greeting for Ivan was, "It's great to be saved! Hallelujah!"

He was alarmed at the unusual response that his warm an spontaneous welcome prompted.

"You are right! It's marvellous to be saved!" Ivan shouted enthusiastically. Then putting his two arms around the astounded evangelist, he lifted him clean off his feet!

"Come on up the Crumlin Road to the prison with me and we will tell them all about it!" he invited, returning Arthur to the safety of the floor.

The normally oozing-with-confidence itinerant preacher was nonplussed at this approach. His spiritual eccentricity had been eclipsed by someone even more eccentric. Anybody who thought that you could just go up to the Crumlin Road prison after eight o'clock on a Sunday evening and preach to the inmates must be out of his mind.

Arthur signalled to one of the busy door stewards to come over. When he did, he instructed, with a gentle firmness, "Show this good man and the lady to a seat, please!"

Ivan and Sylvia were both glad to sit down in their second church service of the evening, though perhaps for slightly different reasons.

The warmth and enthusiasm of that service really appealed to the new convert. Now he appreciated the bright singing. Now he could understand why people were so whole-hearted in their praise to God.

He was too.

Ivan identified with Arthur Blissit. He loved the unqualified sincerity of his preaching, even though some of his proposals were slightly unorthodox by his father's standards. Bible Belfast had always been relatively conservative.

"If you can't preach, hit them with a sticker!" he advocated.

"Let them have it! Stick 'Smile, God loves you,' on their lapel or their car window. Don't be ashamed of it! It's true isn't it? Go for their foreheads if they stand in front of you long enough!"

This travelling preacher did and said things Ivan had never before associated with Gospel ministry.

He was completely spontaneous, but utterly dedicated. A Christian revolutionary.

Ivan liked him. He was "right up his street"!

The now-happily-united-in-Christ couple savoured every moment of that meeting, and decided to walk home afterwards.

Although Sylvia was still experiencing some pain in her feet, the sit-down had helped her, and she was delighted to be with her radically-changed-already husband.

Ivan was simply "walking on air."

How different this walk home was to prove from the one from Queen Margaret Gardens about a month earlier. On that evening Sylvia had been in absolute ecstasy and her husband in total opposition.

Now things were completely changed. Ivan was left to wonder why he had never seen it before.

All those wasted years!

If he had known any Scripture verses he would probably have quoted them that night.

But he couldn't. He didn't know any.

If he had known any hymns he would probably have sung them that night.

But he couldn't/ He didn't know any.

So as they made their way homeward the only way he knew of giving expression to his overwhelming joy was to shout out periodically, "I'm saved, Sylvia! Praise the Lord I'm saved!"

He did this often.

He didn't care who saw him or heard him.

It was great to be free! Genuinely liberated!

No desires left for the 'bookies' or the booze. Not even the 'butts'.

The first thing that met the gaze of this new creation in Christ as he switched on the light in the living room after ten o'clock, was a packet of cigarettes. It had been tossed idly on to the mantelpiece to await Ivan's return for a smoke during 'Moby Dick'!

Picking up the almost-full packet, he walked determinedly over to the window. Then, opening the very same window out of which he had been hanging two weeks before, taunting his praying wife, Ivan tossed it out. Leaning his head against the pane he watched with a glow of satisfaction as it twisted and twirled towards the ground.

They made a cup of tea and sat chatting. They now had common interests. Common goals in life. For the first time in their lives together they were revelling in a fantastic affinity of faith.

There was so much to talk about!

What a night it had been!

Sylvia went to bed around one o'clock in the morning. She was exhilarated by Ivan's conversation but exhausted by all the excitement. Her heels were now in raw flesh.

She had to sleep.

Ivan sat in the living room. He would rap the bedroom wall every now and then.

"Sylvia, love, I'm saved!" he would exclaim.

"Yes, Ivan, I know. It's great!" would come the muffled reply through the half-snores.

"Marvellous. Marvellous. Marvelo ..."

Then she would lapse back into unconsciousness, only to be awakened fifteen or so minutes later by a further wallop on the wall and another exuberant outburst.

Gradually, though, the uninterrupted periods became longer. The whacks on t he wall became less frequent.

As Ivan sat alone in the silence of that cooling room, in the middle of the night, the world of wonder began to wane.

Doubts began to creep into his mind.

Reality was coming closer.

"How can you keep this up?" a little voice whispered. "You above all people.

What about the Brown Horse bar beside your work?

What about the 'bookies' above it?

What about your workmates?

WHAT ABOUT TOMORROW?"

14

First Encounters

It was a drab morning. Monday the first of November.

Ivan was travelling into Belfast city-centre to his work, at the rear of a smoke-filled bus. The back seats of the bus were reserved for smokers, but Ivan wasn't smoking.

That was unusual for him. His first move when he sat down in the bus was always to light up. This morning he just watched the condensation running down the windows and the stale smoke lurking about in the stale air. One or two people whispered to each other. Others looked at folded crumpled newspapers. There was an air of resigned lethargy about the work-bound travellers.

Ivan's mind was in a whirl. All kinds of bewildering questions besieged his reeling brain.

"What will my mates' reaction be when I tell them I have got saved?

What am I going to do when somebody offers me a cigarette?

What will I say when they laugh at me and tell me that it won't last?

And what if it doesn't?"

The recent convert knew nothing of the power of his God to keep, as well as to save. He had no idea of where his strength was going to come from. Nobody had ever attempted to tell him things like that. They thought it would have been a waste of time.

They were right.

That was, of course, up until last night.

That morning in the warehouse was quiet. Monday mornings usually were. Everybody was coming to terms with work, or themselves, after the weekend. Communication took place by a series of grunts. A long grunt, accompanied by a nod of the head, meant "Yes". A short one, with a shake of the head, meant "No".

The big test came at lunch time.

Every day had its own peculiar pattern. As soon as the lunch-break came around, most of the workforce filed into The Brown Horse Bar for a drink. Then when thirsts were satisfied, up they went to the bookies above to place a few bets.

Ivan usually led the way. Today, however, he was hanging back.

"What are you fiddlin' about there for, Ivan?" the foreman enquired, pointedly. "Are you not coming over for a drink?"

Lifting his head to look straight into the other man's eyes, Ivan replied, "I got a cure last night."

"And what was that?" George was puzzled. Must have been some cure, he reckoned, to cure Ivan.

"I became a Christian," Ivan continued, with a calm confidence.

George laughed.

"You shouldn't mimic like that Ivan," he chastened, still laughing. "It's not right to do that, you know!"

"I'm not mimicking Geordie," was the positive reply. "I have become a Christian."

The foreman gave his own leg a light-hearted smack. Then, pointing a finger at his workmate, he chuckled incredulously, "You mean, YOU - HAVE- TURNED - RELIGIOUS!"

"I mean, I - HAVE - GOT - SAVED!" Ivan retorted, with genuine conviction.

"He has got saved! He has got saved!"

Geordie walked round in a circle, guffawing in glee. Then he called to a few of the others who hadn't yet made it to The Brown Horse.

"Did you hear the latest? Ivan Thompson has got saved!"

A bantering session followed.

Standing in silence, the young Christian listened to them. They were all at it now!

"How long will we give him?" they taunted.

After some further ridicule they decided that "the whole notion" would have gone off him in six weeks. And they told him so.

"We will give you six weeks, and then you will be coming with us again. You'll see!" one of them announced. With that they trooped off to The Brown Horse. A good laugh was great for brightening up a dismal day, but it made you thirsty!

Ivan was left alone, to contemplate.

Now he was saved, AND satisfied.

The ice had been broken!

It hadn't been nearly as bad as he had feared. Unknown to him God had given him the words to say when he had to speak, and the wisdom to know when to keep quiet.

Later on in that same week, when Ivan had succeeded to some degree in establishing a Christian testimony, and his workmates had succeeded in accepting it, his next test came.

It was morning-tea time. Men were standing or sitting around chatting to one another. Some were sipping tea or coffee. Some were smoking.

A different George was leaning against a pile of boxes, sucking a pipe. He seemed to spend more time sucking at his unlit pipe than he did actually smoking it.

Removing the extinct volcano from his mouth, and cupping it tenderly in his hand, he spoke directly to Ivan.

"How do you know you are saved?" he asked, suddenly.

Ivan's mind went totally blank. He had no databank of Bible verses stashed away in his subconscious, for such a situation. He didn't KNOW any Scripture verses. Not a one.

All eyes were instantly focused on their one-time drinking companion. Now there was a good question. How was he going to answer that?

Ivan knew that they were all just waiting for his reply. It was going to be very important.

Seeking to buy time, he returned the question to sender.

"How do you know that you are NOT?" he retorted.

George was stumped. He pushed his cap back as he rubbed his forehead.

"I know rightly I'm not," he said, after a few moments delay.

"Well then, that's how I know that I am," Ivan was pleased to continue. "I know rightly that I am."

Not to be outdone, George came on the offensive again, later on that same day.

It was lunchtime. They were all crowded into the little lunch-room. Just as the thick rubber bands cut from old car tubes, were being stretched back over their dented tin boxes, and before the pilgrimage for some to The Brown Horse, there came the second query. Surely this one would prove unanswerable!

"How do you know there's a God, Ivan?" he enquired. There was a smirk of confidence on his face which meant, "You won't wriggle out of this! Got you now!"

"That's easy," Ivan responded, immediately. "No problem. I know there's a God because I was talking to Him this morning!"

There was a short silence in the lunch-room and Ivan decided to press home his point. "And what's more, George," he went on, "we were talking about YOU!"

That was enough for George. He didn't want to hear any more of this religious stuff. Some filtered off to the pub. Others changed the subject.

Once again Ivan was left with his thoughts, and a heart that was praising God.

Salvation brought many blessings into Ivan's life. It brought a deep-seated peace, a sense of purpose, and a hitherto almost unknown harmony at home.

One thing that this wonderful change in his life brought with it also, however, was an awakened conscience in relation to wrongs of the past. Some of these it would be impossible to rectify, he knew. More recent misdemeanours, though, he could do something about.

Over the past months in his employment, he had taken items, mainly tools, belonging to his employer. These he either kept for himself, or sold off to his friends to make a few shillings extra for the bookies.

Now his conscience troubled him. He was a Christian and had no desire to pilfer from his employer again, but he also wanted to make restoration, somehow, for the goods he had taken.

Thus it was that on a Friday morning, almost two weeks after that memorable night in Abbot's Cross Congregational Church, Ivan climbed the stairs to the office of Mr. John Lowry, managing director of Kennedy and Morrison Ltd. He was afraid for the outcome of such a meeting. He might get the sack, but he had to tell the boss how he felt!

When he knocked gently on the door, a man's voice called, "Come in!"

Ivan opened the door and entered.

Mr. Lowry sat back in the chair at his desk, and looking at his employee standing nervously before him, said without preamble, "If it's a pay rise you are after, the answer is NO!"

"It's not a pay rise that I want to see you about, sir," Ivan replied, meekly.

The boss allowed his face to crease into a smile. "All right then, please take a seat," he said.

Ivan sat down on the only other chair in the office, but he didn't know how to approach his main reason for being there. So he talked about other things. The weather, how he liked his work, the pleasant decor of the manager's office.

Mr. Lowry was a busy man, and he was also rather astute. As a general rule his employees didn't come up to see him in the middle of a working day for chummy little chats. There would be something behind this visit.

"What is it, Ivan?" he asked at length. "Why have you come up to see me?"

"Well, it's just like this, Mr. Lowry." Ivan was glad to get started on the real business of the day. "I just want to thank you for giving me a job without knowing anything about my background. It was very kind of you and I appreciate it. But I have a confession to make. Over this last six or nine months or so I have been taking things, I mean stealing things, out of the firm. I have become a Christian now and I have just come up to say how sorry I am..." He let his voice tail away. A short break would allow him to gauge Mr. Lowry's reaction to what he had said so far.

Would he get the sack?

Would he reach for the telephone?

Would he send for the police?

He did none of these things. Instead, he just sat there, deep in thought. As Ivan watched his face, he noticed the tears welling up in the boss's eyes. When they began to overflow on to his cheeks he whisked them away quickly with a finger.

Eventually he managed to put his thoughts into words.

"Thank you, Ivan," he replied, gratefully, graciously. "I'm quite sure that you are not the first one to take something from me. But you are the first person to come and confess it. Thanks again for being so decent."

That gave Ivan the opportunity to introduce the next stage of his prepared plan. "I would like to make some kind of an arrangement so that I can pay you back all that I owe you," he volunteered.

Mr. Lowry rose to his feet. The smile had returned to his face and his hand was extended to shake that of his suddenly-become-honest employee.

"Don't worry about that, Ivan. Don't worry about a thing." His tone was reassuring. "There won't be another word about it."

Leaving that office, Ivan felt that he could have jumped down all the stairs at one mighty leap. He felt so happy. So relieved.

Yet another load had been lifted.

To make his bundle of blessings complete, when he opened his pay packet the following week, he discovered that he had been given the pay rise which he had told his employer he wasn't asking for!

Ivan was beginning to prove, early in his Christian experience, that his God was able to do immeasurably more than all he could ask for, or even imagine.

But he had never heard of Ephesians chapter three verse twenty!

15

The Secret Of Success

Now that Ivan was saved, and Sylvia was saved, they were satisfied. Satisfied that is in the fact that they were at peace with God, and with each other.

This salvation, however, that brought them such tranquility of mind and spirit, brought with it also an insatiable desire to know more. More, more, much more.

"More, more about Jesus."

They attended an evangelical meeting, somewhere, every night of the week.

When they went into the city centre now, it wasn't to visit the bookmakers' shops. It was to browse in the Bethel bookshop!

The transformation was total!

Linda Wright, who had been such a help to Sylvia, in her early days as a Christian, now became a spiritual mother to both of them. She had doubled her flock!

It was with Linda's encouragement that the young couple began to attend the weekly ministry meetings in Fortwilliam Gospel Hall. How they looked forward to those meetings! They just couldn't get enough of it. As spiritual babes they had an endless thirst for the "sincere milk of the Word."

And they were growing!

One of the speakers who came to the Fortwilliam Gospel Hall was Mr. Archie Carew. When Ivan and Sylvia heard that this well-known speaker from London was coming to teach Church principles, they determined that they wouldn't miss a night.

They didn't either! Every single night they were there, Bible and notebook with them. They just wanted to learn as much as they could, as quickly as they could, about their newly found faith.

On one of those evenings, Archie Carew spoke about believer's baptism.

The Lord spoke to Ivan. This was something that he thought he must do. He must be baptised. He wanted to be identified with Christ, in every possibly way. Hadn't it been pointed out from the Bible that this was a Scriptural command and practice?

A few nights later, Ivan approached an elder of the assembly, a man whom he knew, called Joe Arnold.

"Joe, I hope you don't mind me asking you, but Sylvia and I would like to be baptised. How do we go about getting it arranged?" he enquired.

"Delighted to hear it, brother! Delighted to hear it!" was the older man's response. "Don't worry about it. Leave the arrangements to me."

Thus it as that Ivan and Sylvia met with the elders of Fortwilliam Gospel Hall, and their baptism, by immersion, was organised.

What a night of rejoicing their baptism turned out to be! Now they were beginning to scratch at the surface of a mountain of spiritual truth that they had never even dreamed existed, six months before.

Buried with Him by baptism into death.

Raised to walk in newness of life.

Wonderful, wonderful stuff!

Before their conversion they had no time for church services. No time for singing hymns. No time for Christians.

Now they were surrounded by Christians, in a Church meeting, praising God in hymn singing and being obedient to the Lord's command.

What a hallowed experience!

Something else for which Ivan had a lot of time now, was prayer.

The man who used to mock his wife for her sincere but simple prayers, wanted to pray to his loving, caring Heavenly Father, any time he could.

Somebody somewhere had explained to him that through the Bible God could talk to him. Through prayer he could talk to God.

Ivan made the most of both opportunities!

One Friday night he decided to go along to the all-night prayer meeting in Abbot's Cross Congregational Church. One of his Christian friends had told him that a number of dedicated believers met there "to seek God's face in blessing" as they put it, in fervent earnest prayer throughout the night.

Ivan wondered, at first, how anybody could pray all night, but if those old men up there could do it, so could he. He was a lot younger then most of them. He would go and bail them out!

On entering the prayer meeting room. Ivan was gland to see a familiar face. It was Jimmy Carson. The man who had paraded him up to the front of the Church on his very first night, now beamed with pleasure to see him attending the all night prayer meeting.

For his very first night!

Ivan went over and sat, then knelt, beside him.

As the prayer meeting got under way the young man was touched by the sincerity of these mature Christians. They prayed from their hearts, about something that really mattered to them. They wanted to see unsaved people - dozens - hundreds of them, brought to the Saviour.

When Ivan decided to pray, about an hour into the meeting, he went off like a rocket from a launch-pad. All fire and speed and noise.

After ten minutes, however, he had petered out. The fire became a flicker, the roar became a purr, and the speedometer dropped back to zero.

He had stopped! Dried up! Run out of things to say!

There seemed to be an awful lot of the night left, as well!

At ten to three in the morning Iv an sustained a resounding dig in the ribs. It was Jimmy Carson.

Leaning his mouth over towards the younger man's ear, Jimmy said in a stage whisper, "You'd be better to slip off home to bed, son, and get a wee sleep. Your snoring is disturbing the meeting!"

"O.K. Thanks," Ivan said, wakening up and feeling groggy, stupid and ashamed.

He stood up, stumbled out and went home to bed!

His zeal for things spiritual didn't match up to the maturity of Jimmy Carson and Co. - not yet anyway!

At a Thursday evening service in Fortwilliam Gospel Hall it was announced that on the following Sunday an aged Christian would tell his life story, having been saved for fifty years.

This struck Ivan.

Fifty years! He hadn't even been saved for fifty weeks.

Sylvia and he resolved that they wouldn't miss that meeting. They would love to hear what the man had to say.

The speaker on the Sunday evening was a small, frail old man. When he began to speak, however, Ivan recognised someone who had lived his life in communion with God. Everyone in that crowded hall was held spellbound as the little man recounted his experiences in the Christian life.

It hadn't been "roses, roses all the way."

It hadn't been one long victory song - an endless "Hallelujah chorus."

There had been times of trial and difficulty.

There had been highs and lows. Hills and valleys. Ups and downs.

But always there had been God. His presence, power and faithfulness seemed very real to the speaker.

"I have let God down many a time, I'm ashamed to confess," he said at one stage, "but He has never let me down once. Not once."

Ivan was deeply impressed by this servant of God. His humility. His faith. His genuine love for the Lord.

And for fifty years!

When the meeting was over, Ivan and Sylvia were standing outside the Hall, in a straggling bus queue, in the pouring rain. The umbrellas were up and the coat collars were up.

It was cold, and wet, and miserable.

As they stood there, chatting, Ivan noticed the little preacher-man coming along the footpath towards them.

Speaking hurriedly to his wife, Ivan said, "Sylvia, I want to ask this wee man something. Back in a minute."

With that he broke away from the bus queue and followed the trio who had just passed them. Two taller men with umbrellas were escorting the speaker along the pavement. All three wore overcoats and hats.

Catching up with them was simple. They weren't going fast.

"Excuse me sir, " Ivan began, when he reckoned that he was within earshot. "Could I ask you a question?"

The two men with the umbrellas turned their heads quickly. The older man stopped, and turned himself round, slowly.

"Yes, What is it?" the speaker was as gracious in the street in the rain, as he had been on the platform in the meeting.

"Well, you see I'm not long out of prison. In fact, I'm not that long saved either," the enquiry began. "I was just wondering if you could tell me in a word or two, what is the secret of fifty years in the Lord. I would just love to live for Him for fifty years if I could."

Beckoning with a gloved hand the old man said, "Bend your ear down, son."

Ivan, who had been towering over the smaller man, did as he was told.

Then in a feeble voice that was trying to compete with the drumming of the rain on the black umbrellas, the secret came.

"It is simple, son. It is just this," he revealed.

"Pilgrim bound for the heavenly land,
Never lose sight of Jesus."

With that he turned away again, the brolly-bearers resumed their protective positions, and the three of them moved off into the dripping darkness.

Sylvia was eagerly awaiting her husband's return to the bus queue. She made no effort to curb her interest.

"Well," she asked, enthusiastically, "what did he say? What did he tell you?"

Ivan had been slightly disappointed. He had been expecting some deep and marvellous spiritual utterance. A string of Bible references. Seven points perhaps, all beginning with P, or C or D. Even a five-minute-synopsis of Second Corinthians.

It hadn't been like that.

"Do you know what he said to me, Sylvia? Do you know all he said?" Ivan replied, flatly. The flatness in his voice mirrored the flatness in his spirit.

"Do you know what he said was the secret of his success? Fifty years in the Christian life.

'Pilgrim bound for the heavenly land, Never lose sight of Jesus.'

That was it, Sylvia. That was all. That was what he said.

'Pilgrim bound for the heavenly land,

Never lose sight of Jesus.'"

In his immature fervour, his quest for some profound proclamation, Ivan was unable to appreciate the depth of meaning obtained in those two simple lines.

He does now.

16

It's A Bomb!

It was mid-morning, Tuesday 15 February, 1972.

Ivan was walking along Union Street, just outside Kennedy and Morrison's where he worked. He met one of his workmates, who, like himself, had been crossing from one department to another.

They stood for a moment or two, chatting in the street.

As they talked, three men passed them. One of the three was carrying a parcel. Ivan and his friend took no notice. People were carrying boxes and parcels about in that street all the time. It as what you expected around a hardware stockists.

The three men had gone into the main office of their employers.

When the man who had been carrying the parcel set it down on the office counter, one of his accomplices shouted, "It's a bomb!"

They rushed out into the street and ran away. The entire staff of the establishment rushed out after them.

Pandemonium ensued.

Employees were scuttling away like frightened mice. They ran for a bit, then stopped, panting, and looked back.

There was an echoing boom. The bomb had gone off. A fire started. Within seconds it was an inferno.

By now sirens were wailing. A host of policemen and firemen all seemed to appear at once.

The policemen controlled the panic stricken people in the surrounding streets. They evacuated the buildings, pushed the by-standers back to a safe distance, erected road blocks.

Firemen were playing their hoses on the fire. They were very organised. Some were dousing the flames from ladders. Others were preparing additional hoses or locating fresh water supplies.

There was a solitary figure standing apart from he hushed and awe-struck crowd. He wasn't behind the police cordon. He hadn't been asked to move back.

It was Mr. Lowry.

He had worked in the firm since coming out of school. His first, his only, employment had been with Kennedy and Morrison. He had come up through all the different grades in the company. Now he was managing director.

A white handkerchief came out. Tears were slowly wiped away.

Piercing fingers of flame shot out of the windows and pointed accusingly at the sky. The whole scene was engulfed in choking, billowing smoke.

There were shouts of the firemen and the hiss of steam as water met fire.

Suddenly there was an almighty crash.

The roof had caved in!

A shower of sparks burst outward and upward, twirling about in the air, then disappearing forever.

The worst of the fire was over now.

Kennedy and Morrison Ltd., was an empty, hollow, black and smouldering shell.

Mr. Lowry turned away. There was little left to see. His shoulders were drooped. His heart was broken.

The onlookers felt so sorry for him. He appeared so desolate. He must have felt so despondent.

Mr. Lowry had just lost his life's work.

And Ivan had just lost his job!

17

Do You Know Where You're Going?

After that tragic day for Kennedy and Morrison's, Ivan tried a number of jobs. He couldn't settle in any of them, however.

His burning desire was to tell others about his Saviour. He had been asked to speak in a few evangelistic services at various locations. It would be wonderful to be able to travel to these different places himself, without having to fit in with public transport schedules, or rely on others to give him a lift.

Ivan had always fancied himself as a driver. So he learnt to drive, and not long after passing his driving test procured a job as a van driver with a firm of electrical wholesalers in Belfast.

This was ideal. After driving the van for his deliveries during the day, Ivan was permitted to take it home for his own use in the evenings.

When he had been working for the firm for about six months, Ivan's father made a suggestion to him one day.

"Would you be allowed to use your van at the weekends?" he began. "I would really like to go to Dublin and visit an old friend of mind. Jim Hadnett he's called. Do you remember him Ivan? He is blind, you know."

Yes, Ivan did remember him. And yes, he could only but ask for permission to use the van.

When he asked his immediate boss, Mr. Dennis Campbell, about the possibility of using the van for a weekend excursion, Ivan was wholeheartedly granted approval for his proposed outing.

What Dennis Campbell possibly didn't realise at the time, was that this trip to Dublin was going to be a family affair!

After a few weeks of careful planning and eager anticipation the Saturday excursion-south-of-the-border-day arrived. There were seven of them turned up, all ready for the road.

Ivan was driver. Sylvia was first-mate. Dad was navigator. Four others just came along for the ride. Big weekend out for all!

The journey south, through Banbridge, Newry, Dundalk and Drogheda was a pleasant light-hearted affair. There was much chorus-singing, an occasional shout of "Praise the Lord!" and plenty of good-natured banter.

When they eventually arrived in Dublin everyone was hungry. Very hungry.

"I'm starvin'," was how one of the little old ladies described her prolonged lack of sustenance.

As they approached the city-centre, Ivan spotted what looked to be a suitable restaurant.

"Look," he said, slowing down and pointing. "There's a nice looking place over there. And there's plenty of room to park outside it too."

They all agreed that it looked like "a good place to get a bite to eat." Anywhere would have suited most of them, they were so hungry.

Everyone piled out of the van on to the pavement. It made a welcome change to be out stretching in the fresh air. The van had been great for getting them that far, but conditions inside could hardly have been described as either 'spacious' or 'luxurious.'

The restaurant lived up to their expectation. Everybody had a satisfying meal, and they all seemed to be enjoying the friendly, relaxed, almost holiday atmosphere.

When they were moving out towards the door, and had stopped to pay the bill, the mood changed dramatically. And rapidly.

Ivan pulled across the net curtains on the lower window to glance out on to the street. He might as well just do a quick check on the van, while waiting for the others.

He stared. He stood transfixed. Then when he had recovered sufficient strength in his shaking legs he moved over beside his father. Leaning across, he whispered into his ear, "Don't alarm the rest of them, but the van's away."

Don't alarm the rest of them!

Ivan's dad opened his mouth and yelled, "The van's away! The van's away!"

He rushed over to the window and peered out. Not content with that, he opened the door and dashed out. He was followed by Ivan, then Sylvia, then all the others, at speeds relative to their age and state of mind.

It was true! The van WAS away!

Two empty crisp-bags chased each other in an eddy of wind across the otherwise vacant space where once their van had been parked.

"What will we do now? What are we going to do?" Ivan's father appeared more upset than his very-worried son.

"Well, let's start by phoning the police," Ivan decided.

The restaurant manager, who, unless he had been a totally insensitive person, couldn't have missed the commotion, had the situation well in hand.

"I have phoned the Gardai for you," he volunteered, when Ivan re-entered the restaurant to request that he do just that very thing.

About fifteen minutes later, a car drove up. Two Garda officers got out and came into the restaurant

Ivan went over to them

"It's my van that has disappeared," he offered. "I presume that it is me you are looking for."

"Yes it is," one of them said, "We need some details from you."

Then he began to ask questions. Make of van? Year? Registration number? Colour?

As Ivan gave the answers, the officer was methodically recording them on a foolscap sheet he was holding on a clip-board. On noticing that he was half-way down the second sheet, a query arose in Ivan's mind.

"Is that all the cars that have been stolen this week?" he enquired, after he had supplied all the information requested.

A faint, ironic smile crossed the Garda officer's face.

"This week?!" he repeated softly. "This is a list of all the cars and vans that have been stolen today!"

Ivan was shocked. He stood open-mouthed in amazement. TODAY! And it was still only lunch time!

The second officer, who had been listening to the same old questions with a silent resignation, spotted the fleeting look of terror as it flashed across Ivan's face.

"Don't worry." His first words were reassuring. "We will get it back for you." Then he added, "Eventually."

The clip-board cop wasn't so sure.

"May be," he cautioned, "May be. Remember, it's from the North."

Then, turning to address the whole bewildered party, rather than Ivan specifically, he went on, "Never mind. The van will probably turn up sometime, right enough. In the meantime though, we will take you all to your boarding-house tonight. Then we will pick you up and leave you to the Belfast train in the morning."

Ivan was becoming edgy. His impatience was conceived in frustration.

"Thanks. You can take the rest of these people to our boarding-house if you like," he stormed. "But my wife and I won't be going. We are going out to find the van!"

The Gardai looked at each other. They were both amused and astonished. What kind of 'Northern nuts' were these?

"Do you know where you are going? Have you ever been to Dublin before?" one of them asked, incredulously.

"Yes, I do know where I'm going," Ivan retorted. He was well warmed up by now. "I am going to find our van. The Bible says, 'Seek and ye shall find.' We are going out to seek. We will find that van, you make no mistake!"

With that he grabbed Sylvia by the arm and propelled her towards the door. There was just one more thing left to say. Just one unanswered query.

Looking back over his shoulder, with the open door in his other hand he rounded off the conversation with, "And as for your second question.

No. We have never been to Dublin before. And what's more, we will never be back!"

After Ivan had expressed his sentiments of the moment as forcefully as he could, the pair stamped out on to the street. Two rather baffled Garda officers were left to take the suddenly-solemn remaining five to their 'lodging house,' as they called it, wherever it was, however they liked.

Ivan and Sylvia had only one concern. It was their sole objective. They had to find that van!

As they tramped up one street and down another, up another street and down yet another, Ivan's mood swung between two extremities.

There was the mood of calm assurance.

This was when he kept reassuring himself, the Scripture says, "Seek and ye shall find." We are praying and seeking, so the van will be found. It just had to be found. He had told the Gardai that it would be found, had he not?

Then there was an alternative, not so tranquil mood.

It was the blind panic mood. The fear-of-Monday mood.

When in this frame of mind he kept inventing excuses, anticipating Monday morning.

"Oh yes, Dennis. The van. Well, you see, the van is still down in Dublin somewhere. We just had to leave it there. No. No. I don't know who is using it just at this minute ..."

Still they trudged on. Up and down, up and down, at random. They tried not to cover the same street twice. That wasn't too difficult. There were plenty of streets to choose from.

They didn't talk much.

They were too mixed up. Too tired. Too scared.

After having walked for miles, or so it seemed, and when they were about three-quarters of an hour out from the restaurant, they spotted it.

Yes. It was the van!

Like Rhoda, who went to open the door to Peter in the Bible, they just couldn't credit it at first.

They had been praying ever so hard that the van would be found. Now their prayers had been answered. And they could hardly believe it!

The red van had been abandoned - one could hardly describe it as 'parked,' on a patch of waste ground at a street corner.

Slowly they walked up to it. Was it O.K.? Would anything be stolen.? At least it was there. They had prayed, and sought and found.

Ivan pushed the sliding-door across, and peered inside. Nothing appeared to have been damaged. There wasn't anything stolen, either, as far as he could see. The big Arthur-Blissit-style-sticker that Ivan had stuck on the windscreen, as his trade-mark, smiled down on the enormously relieved couple.

It said, "New Life in Jesus."

They were so thrilled that God had answered their prayer, Ivan and Sylvia got down on their knees beside the van and thanked God for leading them to it.

Then a thought crossed Sylvia's mind. "We'd better not touch it any more, Ivan," she said thoughtfully. "We will phone the Gardai again. They will probably want to take fingerprints."

Having asked at a nearby house for the use of a telephone, Ivan contacted the Gardai, again.

Ten minutes later, while the young couple were still marvelling at God's guidance as they walked round and round the van, a Garda car drew up.

It was the same two officers!

As they emerged from the car, chatting to each other, they looked amazed. It was unbelievable!

One of them took off his cap. Then he scratched his head. "You talk about the luck of the Irish!" he exclaimed.

"That wasn't luck! That was the Lord!" Ivan began. He never missed an opportunity to witness to his faith

"Do you see that sticker on t he windscreen there? It says, 'New Life in Jesus'. The One who found that van, can find you. He is looking for you just now. Jesus came into the ...."

One of the men became rather uneasy. Holding up a hand to stop Ivan in mid-sentence, he interrupted with, "Look, we are awful glad you found the van. But my mate and me will have to go now. There are thefts and murders and all sorts of things going on in this city today. We don't have a lot of time to stand about here."

Having said that, he didn't even wait for any response. Turning on his heel he made for the 'safety' of his car. His companion followed.

They had heard enough from, and seen enough of, that religious freak from the North!

As they drove away, without even so much as a backward glance, Ivan remarked to Sylvia, "So much for your fingerprints!"

They laughed together! Relaxation had returned.

They had found the van, undamaged. That was all they had been worried about.

Now they had to find the guest house where the others would already be, hopefully.

That proved to be easier said than done.

There were two basic problems. And they were big ones.

They didn't know where they were. Number one.

And they didn't know where they were going. Number two.

All they had was an address.

However, after driving up a few blind alleys, and asking a number of pedestrians of all ages, they eventually located the guest house where they had booked to stay the night!

What a night of rejoicing that turned out to be! The crestfallen five, who had spent more than two hours praying silently, and worrying loudly, by turns, were overjoyed to see Ivan and Sylvia return in the van.

The tired but triumphant couple were delighted to see them too.

So they praised God together well into the night.

During the evening, Ivan remembered a verse in Psalm 32. He reminded the others of it.

It said, "I will instruct you and teach you in the way you should go. I will guide you with my eye."

Yes. There had been times when they hadn't known where they were going, but He had known where they needed to go. He had "guided them with His eye."

So precise was His guidance, that it led them to a lost van in a large city!

18

Good News, Bad News

As Ivan continued with his daily deliveries for Taylor's electrical wholesalers, he made many friends, in many stores and companies across the Province. One such friend was Mr.. Blakely, warehouse manager at Hodge Office Supplies.

One day, just as Ivan was leaving the warehouse, having completed his delivery, he remarked, almost casually, to Mr. Blakely, "There wouldn't be a chance of a wee job in here sometime would you think? You're not looking for a van driver or anything like that, are you?"

Since he had merely posed a tentative question, Ivan was quite startled by the answer. "As a matter of fact we are looking for a van driver. Would you be interested?" Mr. Blakely replied.

"Yes, I think I would," Ivan said.

"Leave it with me," the obliging manager offered. "I will have a word with someone about it."

True to his promise, Mr. Blakely did speak to one of his bosses about Ivan, with the end result that Ivan changed jobs, again. He moved to Hodge Office Supplies as a driver in 1975.

It was a sad break to leave Taylor's. Ivan was particularly sorry to say 'Goodbye' to Dennis Campbell, who had been so kind to him. They parted firm friends, on their knees, with Ivan commending his former employer to the Lord.

Whilst delivering office furniture during the day for his new employers served to earn money to pay the bills, Ivan's increasing interest in preaching the Gospel in various churches and meeting-places in the evenings became the sole occupation of his leisure time. He had a burning desire to see people brought to the Saviour, who had made such a marvellous change in all aspects of his life.

Again, transport to meetings was no problem. His employers were very supportive of his desire to preach the Gospel and teach the Scriptures.

The eager preacher's first mission was in Ballybeen, a housing estate in Dundonald, on the outskirts of Belfast. A Christian friend of his, with a like concern for witnessing to others, Wesley Graham, had erected a portable hall there, and asked Ivan to join him.

It was early in 1977. It was winter. It was very cold.

On the first night of their mission, at two minutes to eight o'clock when they were due to commence their service on the hour, there were only three elderly women whom they didn't know, in the hall.

Ivan was discouraged. This was his first real mission. He had imagined a Pentecost experience, right from the start. Perhaps he hadn't really expected three thousand though. He would have settled for three hundred.

Or may be even thirty.

But three!

Trying to hide his disappointment, he asked Wesley. "Which of us is going to speak first here?"

"You are!" was his friend's emphatic reply.

"But how can I get up there and preach to three old women?" Ivan asked. He was only half-hearted because he was down-hearted.

"Do you KNOW these 'three old women' as you call them?" Wesley enquired.

"No, I don't," Ivan confessed.

"Well then, they might not be Christians. Get up there and preach the Gospel to them," was the advice he received.

As he mounted the platform, more people came in, and the service began.

That evening was the first of many. More people heard about the mission and started to attend.

Ivan obtained a lasting blessing from Ballybeen. It was there that his deep-rooted desire for earnest evangelism began to grow, and bud, and bloom. It was there that he experienced the inexplicable joy of presenting the claims of Christ to people over a prolonged period of time.

It was great. Very satisfying. It created an appetite for more.

Two further missions were to follow. One in Castlegore. Some of Ivan's friends thought that he was just ever so slightly daft to travel away to these "wee country places" to preach.

"Where's that place you are now, Ivan?" they taunted him, good-naturedly. "Castle-what?"

"Castle-what" was followed by Cairncastle, outside Larne.

In both these places, there were discouragments. Some were sceptical.

"Nobody has ever had a successful mission there," they said.

"It's the wrong time of the year," they said.

"The people there just aren't interested," they said.

"Mr. So-and-So preached there for seven weeks, and nothing happened," they said.

But the power of God was to prove greater than the predictions of men.

As Ivan persisted in both these "wee country places", preaching in the evenings, after a day's work, blessing was experienced. A strong bond of fellowship was forged between the part-time preacher and the local Christians, who helped and encouraged him.

Here again, despite the 'downers' there were times of rejoicing. Times of prayer were followed by sessions of praise.

God blessed the presentation of His Word.

People who came for a first night out of curiosity, came back by choice, and came to Christ by conviction.

This was inspiration for Ivan. Things were going well. People were attending his meetings and being blessed, Christians were rallying to support him, he was receiving more and more invitations to preach in more and more different locations ...

Then came a temporary set back. It seemed that since things were progressing so favourably, there was an evil force contriving to thwart the effort in every, or any, way.

One Sunday evening, Ivan and Sylvia were travelling home from a meeting in Castlederg. It had been a well-attended service, and they were happy. Ivan had been invited to conduct a mission in the village at a later date.

The signs were good, the prospects bright.

As they were passing through the village of Drumquin, however, the van suddenly went out of control on a bend. They were to discover later that particular bend had often been described as 'an accident black-spot'.

The van went straight across the road, struck a bank and somer-saulted, ending upside down, with wheels in mid-air, in a field.

When they eventually came to rest, Ivan and Sylvia's immediate concern was for each other. When each had established that the other was at least alive, and conscious, though injured, they crawled out into the field. They were afraid of the van catching fire.

Sylvia was too badly hurt to move, so Ivan, though badly cut and shaken, left her in the field and went back to seek help.

On reaching the roadside he frantically waved down a passing motorist. The driver was a lady who had just attended the meeting which he had conducted in Castlederg. She was not a little surprised to find 'the preacher', splattered with mud and caked with blood, standing by the roadside.

Between them they helped Sylvia into the car and the three of them left the scene to go to Omagh Hospital. Sylvia, being more seriously injured had to be detained overnight, but Ivan was released after fragments of glass had been removed from his back.

On leaving the Hospital, Ivan was taken to Omagh Police station to report the details of the accident. By now, news of their misadventure had spread through the local Christian community.

Everyone was deeply concerned.

Rev. David Fletcher, in whose church Ivan had taken the service, was a genuine help and real tower of strength to him, accompanying him to the Police station to make his statement. David seemed to know just how Ivan was feeling, and yet was sufficiently experienced to advise him on what to say and do.

When the police officers had taken all the necessary particulars, David suggested that Ivan should contact his employers. This, he argued quite reasonably, would be only right and proper and Christian. Ivan should report the state of the van, and explain his expected non-attendance at work the next morning.

Ivan agreed with him. Yes. It probably would be the proper course of action, but he had to admit also that the prospect of it didn't exactly fill him with delight.

Since it had to be done, he phoned Mr. Eric Hodge, at home.

"Hello, Eric, this is Ivan," the conversation began, "I am ringing from Omagh Police station. I have some good news for you and some bad news."

It was late on a Sunday night to receive this kind of phone call. Eric's voice was flat and resigned when he responded.

"What's the bad news?" he asked.

"I'm really very sorry about his, but the bad news is that the van is lying on a field on its roof. We skidded off the road in Drumquin!" Ivan's answer was brief and to the point.

There was a slow intake of breath, then silence, at the other end of the line.

In a minute Eric's voice returned, acquiescent. He had the second, hopefully more optimistic, question to ask.

"Well, if that's the bad news, tell me then, Ivan, what is the good news?"

"The good news is that I'm here to tell you. And although Sylvia is in Hospital they have told me that she is going to be O.K."

Eric Hodge was very gracious. He realised that whatever it was that had happened must have been a terrifying experience.

Within seconds he replied, calmly, "If you are here to tell me, and Sylvia's going to be all right, then that must be good news."

Sylvia was released from Hospital after a few days. Ivan's injuries kept him off work for two weeks.

When he did return to work it was with a certain apprehension.

What would his bosses say? Would they 'take him off the road'? Worse still, would they 'show him the door'?

His unease proved totally unfounded. Ivan greatly appreciated the considerate Christian attitude of his employers, who were, in fact, at heart, fellow-labourers with him in the Gospel.

When he returned to work, Hodge Office Supplies had purchased a new van, which he used for his daily deliveries, and which he was permitted to use, as before, for his preaching engagements in the evenings.

No amount of hardship or trial could divert Ivan from his desire to present the Christian message to the people of Northern Ireland.

God had his servants who would support him. And God Himself was greater than any mountain that Ivan could be asked to climb, or any hazard that could be thrown across his path.

Every time 'the enemy came in like a flood' the Lord provided the boat!

19

What's Wrong With Us?

With Ivan's involvement in the spread of the Gospel and Sylvia's intense interest in Ivan's preaching, there was much joy and unity in their marriage.

"Another soul to Jesus born," Ivan would say humbly, reverently, as they travelled home from a meeting on many an evening. Then they would praise God together, praying for spiritual growth in the new born child of faith.

There was just one distant cloud in their sky, though. A cloud that threatened to drift closer, grow darker and block out the sun.

Like Hannah in the Bible, like a high percentage of women, in fact, Sylvia yearned for a child. A baby would be the crowning blessing on their marriage, she felt.

Ivan was being used to bring spiritual children to Christ. It was delightful to witness new-born babes display the first signs of healthy life in their Lord.

Surely, He would grant them a little baby boy or girl to thrill a mother's heart.

But there were to be problems.

After a number of childless years, Ivan and Sylvia sought medical help.

They attended various clinics over a lengthy period of time. They answered hundreds of questions. They prayed hundred of prayers.

After all the tests had been conducted, all the questions had been answered, and all the prayers had been prayed, the final result came.

The sum and substance of it all was, "No. Sorry. Unfortunately, a child from this marriage will not be possible."

This was a big blow. A big BIG blow. Not a slap-in-the-teeth type sudden blow, but a creeping disappointment that threatened to nibble and nibble away at the core of their otherwise happy partnership.

It was hard to keep back the bitterness. Why, when they switched on the TV at News time did they hear of mothers who didn't seem to want their children? Who neglected them? Left them unattended?

They would never do that!

Why did Ivan's older brother Jim and his wife have children, and his younger brother Roy and his wife have a family too, and he and Sylvia have none?

That was hard to swallow.

Why did it seem that God was being so hard on a young couple who were so dedicated to serving Him and seeking His will for their lives?

They wondered sometimes. They shared their feelings with each other sometimes. It would be useless sharing it with any of their friends, for none of them had experienced the sense of emptiness that was nagging away at their hearts. Or so they thought.

"What's wrong with us? What's wrong with us?" they asked each other time and time again, out of a sense of frustration.

There was no easy answer to that one. So when they didn't get any satisfaction they asked it again, in other forms.

"What have we done to deserve this?" they reflected. Or, "What have we NOT done to deserve this? Have we gone wrong somewhere?"

There was one possible solution to the problem, however. It was a solution suggested repeatedly by doctors and gynaecologists who had been conducting the seemingly endless series of clinics.

"Think seriously about adoption," they kept advising, even before final confirmation of Ivan and Sylvia's inability to have a family.

Sylvia still longed for a child.

"We should apply for adoption, Ivan," she kept hinting to her rather reluctant husband. Ivan wanted a family too, but he had his reservations about such an application.

Sometimes he was tolerant, smiled and said glibly, "Aye. That might be a good idea, Sylvia. We will have to see ..."

Increasingly though he permitted his true feelings to be expressed. His reservations were based on reality.

"Think about it, Sylvia," he would say, frankly, "Just think for ONE minute. Do you honestly believe that when they hear of my background they would allow us to adopt a baby? They don't go handing out babies to jail-birds you know. We may just forget it."

Ivan could have lived with the childlessness, the disappointment and even the gnawing grudge against himself, or his partner, or God, or whoever.

Sylvia couldn't. And she couldn't, and wouldn't 'just forget it.' She wanted a child. She had set her heart upon having a baby to love and cherish and rear.

So she persisted. She just kept on, gently, persuasively. And as the slow but steady dripping of water wears away the rock, and as the constant blows of the axe fell the tree, so her persistence won the day. Sylvia had learnt a simple lesson from that rewarding night when she had half-pushed, half-dragged her totally uncooperative husband into Abbot's Cross Congregational Church.

It was that even big men buckle, eventually.

You only have to keep at it longer.

One day Ivan caved in. He said, "All right, Sylvia. We will give it ago. We have nothing to lose. You get the papers and we will send them away."

Thus it was that they applied for adoption.

Sylvia was pleased. It was what she wanted.

Ivan got a kind of warm glow from it also. It hadn't been a big job to apply. Sylvia was happy. They would never hear another word about it, he was sure.

That would be it.

A few weeks passed. Nothing happened.

Perhaps Ivan was right.

Then they had a letter. A Social worker was coming to visit them. Sylvia was delighted. To her, this was the start of the process, the first rung on the ladder.

Ivan was doubtful. "Hope Sylvia won't be too upset after having her hopes built up, but when the social worker gets a glimpse into my background, what will DEFINITELY be it," he reasoned.

When the social worker arrived, Ivan and Sylvia were all dressed up. This was a big event for them. They had to create a good impression.

The interview began with a number of general introductory questions.

Dates of birth? How long have you been married? Are you both willing to undergo medical examinations? Etc. etc. ...

Ivan stopped him. He didn't want to waste the man's time, or raise their hopes prematurely.

"There are some things which I feel I ought to tell you, before you go any further," he explained.

Resting his pen on the file of sheets and forms before him, the social worker looked up. He was taken somewhat by surprise.

"And what would they be?" he asked, quietly.

"Firstly, I have a prison record," Ivan began, with more feeling than he had intended to display, but he so much wanted to clear the air. "I have done time in the Crumlin Road, But secondly, I am a Christian now. I have been changed by the grace of God."

Ivan paused, waiting for a reaction. There was none, so he continued, "Whether all this makes a difference, or not, to adoption procedures, I don't know. I feel it's only right to make you aware of the situation, though, in case it does."

Having had his say, Ivan stopped. It was all out in the open now.

This was the moment of truth.

Would he say "Oh!" pack up his papers and leave?

No. He didn't.

Would he thank them for being so open about everything, then make some excuse to hurry back to the office?

No. He didn't do that either.

He just continued with his task, taking down more information

"We will put everything down on the forms, here, for consideration. Then we will make up our minds," he remarked, calmly.

As they were leaving him to the door, Sylvia couldn't restrain herself. She had to ask the burning question.

"When will we know whether we have been accepted or not?" She enquired.

"You will get a letter by-and-by," he assured them, and left.

Sylvia was beaming. She just had a baby in her arms.

Ivan was more hopeful. Less doubtful. The door hadn't been slammed in their faces. In fact, if anything, it had opened just a chink.

Then the waiting began.

A week. Two weeks. Nothing. Not a word.

A month. Two months. Nothing. Official silence.

Hope was waning. Despair was growing.

It was almost three months later when the letter came. Just a simple brown envelope, lying in the hall.

Sylvia lifted it. Ripped it open. Quickly she glanced at the letter.

Then she read it again. And then again, just to make sure.

"They are coming back, Ivan!" she exclaimed at length. "They will be back to see us again!"

"They", whoever "They" all were, kept their promise. They came back. Again, and again and again.

It was all to prove worthwhile, however.

As the merry-go-round of interviews and discussions bobbed on and on, the door began to open wider for Ivan.

It was half-open now. Then three-quarters. Light was beginning to stream from the other side.

Hope was mounting.

Was Sylvia's persistence going to prove profitable after all?

Two years, almost to the day, after that first uncertain meeting with the social worker, their greatest joy was realised.

They looked down for the first time on a little six-week old, fair haired baby boy. Sylvia was encouraged to lift him in her arms.

She did so.

As she gently cradled the baby close to her breast, her countenance was a picture.

She was smiling and weeping all at once!

Now she was complete. Now they were complete.

Now they were a family.

Jonathan had arrived.

For six blissful months the new addition increased their happiness an-hundred fold.

Then they had to return to court. They had applied for a legal adoption of little Jonathan.

So Ivan and Sylvia went back to Crumlin Road Courthouse. They were together this time, though, sitting side by side. And their total joy of a tiny boy was with them as well.

It was a different judge, but he looked over his glasses, just as the previous one had done, many years before.

It was a different verdict also. Leaning forward with a caring expression, he announced warmly, "Having considered all aspects of this case, I can see no reason why you as a couple cannot keep this child."

It was an ENTIRELY different verdict!

As they left the courthouse that morning, Ivan held his infant son up in his arms, and dedicated him to God.

Across the road he could just pick out the window of the prison cell where he served his sentence.

He was ashamed of his past of petty crime.

He was rejoicing in his new life in Christ.

He was thrilled with the human life that throbbed in his hands. What a delight!

What a privilege.

What a God!

20

Why Take The Risk?

Jonathan brought much joy to the young couple. He afforded them a unity as a family which they hadn't known before. He was a theme of their prayers and praises, a focus for their love.

Then, when Johnathan was five years old, a further blessing was added to their increasing happiness.

Rachel was adopted also.

Now they had a boy and a girl. One of each. Now there were four of them. Their family was complete.

Ivan and Sylvia felt so satisfied. So blessed.

There was no jealousy now. No wondering, either. No more self-examination.

God had been so good. Ivan and Sylvia had just learnt another lesson.

They had learnt that they must await God's timing, which wasn't always theirs.

Within the family, the busy life continued. Ivan carried on with his established pattern, working by day on his deliveries, and preaching the Gospel in the evening.

The frequency of his speaking engagements had increased, however. Now he was out almost every night of the week, preaching in evangelical groups of all denominations.

He always preached at least twice on a Sunday.

The pressure began to mount. He knew that there would soon come a point where he would be unable, both physically and spiritually, to keep up the pace.

How could he give his employers an honest day's work, and then be fresh in his presentation of the message that he loved to proclaim, every night of the week?

Besides that, now he had added responsibility. Having pleaded with God for a family, he and his wife had to care for them, physically, emotionally , spiritually ...

With all these considerations churning around in his mind, Ivan attended a Faith Mission Convention in Bangor.

The speaker was Mr. Alex Passmore.

The subject was 'The Surrendered Life.'

The Spirit was moving.

At the close of that service, Ivan was convicted. With head bowed down, almost between his knees, and with determination of soul, he made a vow to God.

It was a vow that he was sure he could keep.

The terms of it were simple. It was this.

"If it ever comes to a choice between secular employment or serving God, then God will be given the pre-eminence. It will definitely be 'God first' in my life."

Ivan meant it. He was sincere.

But when the emotional passion of the Convention had passed, he settled into the usual routine again.

Driving, delivering, preaching, driving, delivering, preaching ...

And it was when he was fulfilling one of his many preaching engagements that his vow came bouncing back, to challenge him.

It was a Sunday morning. Ivan was speaking to Christians in Lurgan. The church was almost full.

He had read from Judges chapter eleven in the Bible. It was a story about a man called Jephthah and a vow he had made.

Standing on that platform, speaking to others, Ivan had the strange sensation of experiencing God speaking to him through his own words.

"Have you ever made a vow to the Lord?" he enquired of his audience.

"Have you?" came back the voice of God to his soul.

"If you have, have you kept your vow?" he went on, striving to ignore the call of conscience.

"Have you?" came back the voice of God to his soul.

"Jephthah was prepared to fulfil his vow, even though it was going to mean terrible loss for him. Listen to what the Bible says ...' he continued.

Picking up his Bible, Ivan read aloud, "I have opened my mouth unto the Lord and I cannot go back."

Looking up from his reading, the speaker straightened himself up and pointed down to his congregation.

"Have you opened your mouth to the Lord? Ever? And now have you thought twice about it? Have you gone back on your vow?" Ivan challenged them.

"Have YOU?" came back the voice of God to his soul.

Somehow he got through to the end of that service. No matter what he said to challenge his listeners, he was confronted with it himself.

As the congregation filed out of the church that morning, they assured Ivan that they had "really enjoyed that".

"That was a GREAT message," some of them remarked, earnestly.

Ivan was glad to see they were so pleased about it.

It hadn't been 'GREAT' for him.

He was now forced into contemplation of his future in Christian service.

What should he do?

One thing was for sure. He was not going to do anything in too big a hurry, despite his vow.

He was too content. It was all too cosy. Much too comfortable.

His employers were sympathetic to his Gospel outreach aspirations, even to the extent of allowing him to publish a newsletter, while paying him well for his daily work.

He had the best of both worlds, with no worries about money.

Being in demand as a speaker, and experiencing God's blessing on his ministry, gave him a certain amount of spiritual satisfaction.

Driving a van during the day for a steady wage give him guaranteed financial stability.

He had it made.

Evangelical groups began to 'call' him to come and preach and teach in their churches. They would like him to leave his full time employment and enter a pastorate with them.

But no. He couldn't.

His excuses of, "I don't think I'm ready for that yet," or "There are other better preachers about than me," only thinly veiled the truth which was, "I am far too comfortable the way I am. Thank you very much."

Often, in quiet, late night conversation about his further service for God, Ivan would say to Sylvia, "Why should we take the risk? I am secure in Hodges. Pension and all. I can get as much preaching as I want in the evenings. And I'm nearly killed on a Sunday.

What if I 'step out in faith' and it doesn't work out in practice? What then? I couldn't very well go back to my employers and expect to be given my job again.

Why should we take the risk?"

Sometime later Ivan was invited back to Lurgan, to speak to the Mourneview Assembly people once more.

As he stood there, on that particular Sunday morning, speaking about Moses, he chanced to remark, "Moses was content to dwell with his father-in-law. That was exactly when God called him. When he was content ..."

Ivan continued his address, but it was words from the Lord. He had little control over his speech. His mind was in turmoil. A burning conviction smote his conscience. Again.

"You are preaching to these people about being content," it said. "About God calling Moses. About God calling them. What about yourself? What about God calling YOU? You have turned down many calls to full-time service? Why? Because you are content."

Ivan wrestled with it.

On his way home in the car, he expressed his genuine concerns to his Heavenly Father, in silent prayer.

"Oh God, no, please. Don't ask me to take any risks. I'm not ready for that. There are others more suited to full-time evangelism than me. What about ...?" His mind raced over a number of other Christians he would have rated higher than himself on the ladder of Gospel preachers and Bible teachers.

It was the old "Here I am, send him," philosophy.

But God had his man. God wanted his man.

It seemed to be a further distinct voice from God to Ivan, then, when in 1989 a group of elders and deacons from Mourneview Assembly called to visit him. It had been on the platform of that church that God had challenged him personally. Twice.

When the visiting group got around to stating the purpose of their call, it was quite straight-forward.

"We believe that God has sent us to you. We would like you to come and be Pastor at our church," they stated.

Here was the most direct indication from God yet, of His purpose for Ivan's life. Ivan might have been able to dismiss the other challenges as figments of his imagination or perhaps he could attribute them to an emotional 'high'.

But there was no mistaking this one. There was no way around it!

Here was a group of men, sitting in his living room, saying to him, "We want you to come and preach for us!"

"Leave it with me, " Ivan requested, later in the evening, as the deputation was about to set off for home. "I will think about it seriously and pray about it earnestly."

A week later Ivan received an official call from the church, by letter. There it was in 'black and white'.

He had to do something about it. A firm decision would have to be made, sooner or later.

Sylvia and he spent the summer in prayer and consideration. It would be a giant step into the unknown.

However, the more they prayed about it, and the more they thought about it, they were convinced that it was God's will that Ivan should give up his day-to-day job and serve the Lord in a full-time capacity.

As the deadline which he had set himself for handing in his notice approached, he was beset by doubts.

Driving around the Province at his work, a sneaking voice seemed to whisper to him from time to time, "Ivan, you are still as daft as ever. What are you giving up your good job for? A lot of the chaps that you know would give an arm and a leg for a steady job like this. And you are just about to chuck it all up!

Why are you taking this risk?"

Eventually though, Ivan decided. Carefully, prayerfully, even tearfully, he determined to be true to his own vow.

"God will never let you down," he had told his congregations often.

Now he was being asked to prove it.

It would be God first - at last.

In September, 1989, therefore, Ivan gave notice to his employers that he would be leaving at Christmas. He had formally accepted the call to Mourneview.

Parting with his fellow-workers at Hodge Office Supplies was a painful experience. Ivan had led some of them to the Saviour. They were in a very real sense, his children in Christ. He loved them all.

They must have appreciated their van man's ministry among them., too, for they all clubbed together and bought him a Bible.

Ivan's final act before leaving secure employment was to kneel down together with Mr. Eric and Mr. Stanley Hodge, senior partners in the firm, while they committed the future of their just-about-to-leave employee to the Lord.

In his turn, Ivan praised God for their help and kindness to him, and also sought God's direction for his life.

It was a touching, Christian farewell.

There were to be many niggling doubts in the days to come.

Ivan would have liked cast-iron guarantees.

God didn't give guarantees for a life time though. He gave grace for each step.

If God had given his servant a guarantee of an easy ride for a life time he could have become self-confident.

God gave him grace for each step so that he could become God-reliant.

On 1st January, 1990, Ivan was installed as the Pastor of Mourneview Assembly in Lurgan.

He had 'stepped out' in faith.

He had done what he had wondered about so often. He had 'taken the risk.'

Ivan was to prove in the days to follow that his whole thinking had been all wrong.

His fears were groundless.

An Almighty God doesn't deal in 'risks'. There is no such a thing with Him.

God deals in power and assurance.

In strength and stability.

In provision and protection.

Ivan was relying on a totally reliable God.

He still is!